Robert Allen Cooley

The coccid genera Chionaspis and Hemichionaspis

Robert Allen Cooley

The coccid genera Chionaspis and Hemichionaspis

ISBN/EAN: 9783741130984

Manufactured in Europe, USA, Canada, Australia, Japa

Cover: Foto ©Thomas Meinert / pixelio.de

Manufactured and distributed by brebook publishing software
(www.brebook.com)

Robert Allen Cooley

The coccid genera Chionaspis and Hemichionaspis

SPECIAL BULLETIN.

HATCH EXPERIMENT STATION

OF THE

Massachusetts Agricultural College.

THE COCCID GENERA

CHIONASPIS AND HEMICHIONASPIS.

R. A. COOLEY, B. Sc.

AUGUST 10, 1899.

AMHERST, MASS.:
Press of Carpenter & Morehouse,
1899.

HATCH EXPERIMENT STATION

OF THE

Massachusetts Agricultural College,

AMHERST, MASS.

By act of the General Court, the Hatch Experiment Station and the State Experiment Station have been consolidated under the name of the Hatch Experiment Station of the Massachusetts Agricultural College. Several new divisions have been created and the scope of others has been enlarged. To the horticultural, has been added the duty of testing varieties of vegetables and seeds. The chemical has been divided, and a new division, "Foods and Feeding," has been established. The botanical, including plant physiology and disease, has been restored after temporary suspension.

The officers are :—

HENRY H. GOODELL, LL. D.,	*Director.*
WILLIAM P. BROOKS, PH. D.,	*Agriculturist.*
GEORGE E. STONE, PH. D.,	*Botanist.*
CHARLES A. GOESSMANN, PH. D., LL. D.,	*Chemist* (Fertilizers).
JOSEPH B. LINDSEY, PH. D.,	*Chemist* (Foods and Feeding).
CHARLES H. FERNALD, PH. D.,	*Entomologist.*
SAMUEL T. MAYNARD, B. SC.,	*Horticulturist.*
J. E. OSTRANDER, C. E.,	*Meteorologist.*
HENRY M. THOMSON, B. SC.,	*Assistant Agriculturist.*
RALPH E. SMITH, B. SC.,	*Assistant Botanist.*
HENRI D. HASKINS, B. SC.,	*Assistant Chemist* (Fertilizers).
CHARLES I. GOESSMANN. B. SC.,	*Assistant Chemist* (Fertilizers).
SAMUEL W. WILEY, B. SC.,	*Assistant Chemist* (Fertilizers).
EDWARD B. HOLLAND, M. SC.,	*First Chemist* (Foods and Feeding).
FRED W. MOSSMAN, B. SC.,	*Ass't Chemist* (Foods and Feeding).
BENJAMIN K. JONES. B. SC.,	*Ass't Chemist* (Foods and Feeding).
PHILIP H. SMITH, B. SC.,	*Assistant in Foods and Feeding.*
GEORGE A. DREW, B. SC.,	*Assistant Horticulturist.*
HERBERT D. HEMENWAY, B. SC.,	*Assistant Horticulturist.*
ARTHUR C. MONAHAN,	*Observer.*

The co-operation and assistance of farmers, fruit-growers, horti-culturists, and all interested, directly or indirectly, in agriculture, are earnestly requested. Communications may be addressed to the HATCH EXPERIMENT STATION, Amherst, Mass.

INTRODUCTION.

In the preparation of this paper it was intended to bring together all obtainable information concerning the known species of the genera treated, and to give this information in such form as to be of service to the general entomologist as well as to the specialist.

For the purpose of securing for study as large an amount of material as possible, Professor Fernald prepared and sent out a circular letter to a large number of entomologists both in this country and abroad, and we also sent personal letters to all who were especially interested in the Coccidae, asking for specimens. The results have been most gratifying, for a large amount of material has been received from nearly every correspondent. I also spent some time in Washington studying the unrivaled collection of Coccids in the Department of Agriculture where every facility for this work was granted by Dr. L. O. Howard and his assistants.

It became evident in the course of my work that the genus *Chionaspis* in the sense in which it was first established was an unnatural group and must be broken up into several genera. *Chionaspis* in a restricted sense and *Hemichionaspis* have been treated of in this paper and it is my intention at some future time to publish the others.

The generic name *Chionaspis* has been retained for that division which includes *salicis* L. and this species should be regarded as Signoret's type of the genus, as is shown later in this work, as well as for the genus in its more restricted sense. It may be well to state that the old genus *Chionaspis* now contains over one hundred species, and that not only in my own collection, but also in that of the Massachusetts Agricultural College are authentic specimens of nearly all of these, as well as a very large number of species in other genera of the Coccidae.

I take this opportunity to express my sincere thanks to all who have kindly aided me, either with specimens or otherwise, and especially to Mr. Alexander Craw of San Francisco, Cal. for specimens of very choice species; to Mr. A. H. Kirkland of Malden, Mass. for numerous specimens collected by himself, and to Mr. C. P. Lounsbury, Government Entomologist at Cape Town, South Africa, for a large amount of material from that country. The late Mr. W. M. Maskell before his death very kindly sent specimens of many of his species and also an almost complete set of his publications on the Coccidae. I am also under obligations to Dr. L. Zehntner of Java for copies of his finely illustrated papers on scale insects as well as for examples of his species; to Mr. E. E. Green who has been especially generous in sending specimens of every species of *Chionaspis* known to occur in Ceylon ; to Dr. L. O. Howard who has allowed me every opportunity to study the collection in the Department of Agriculture and also given me much valuable information, and to Prof. T. D. A. Cockerell who has rendered much assistance by sending numerous specimens and by giving valuable information from time to time. Much credit is due Miss Ida J. Russell who has spent many patient hours preparing and mounting these scale insects and has become very proficient in the work. I wish to express my sincere appreciation of the assistance in my studies and in the preparation of this paper, given by Prof. C. H. Fernald, and also of his energy and success in obtaining specimens and literature on the Coccidae as well as for valuable advice and suggestions.

SCALE-INSECTS BY MAIL.

A few words should be said upon the danger of sending scale insects by mail. There is comparatively little danger of the formation of new colonies of scale insects by immature females on detached leaves or branches as these soon wither and die and the scale insects attached to them perish. I have repeatedly received insects in this condition and they soon died and shriveled up. The case is entirely different, however, when scales enclosing eggs or mature viviparous females are sent. Species of the subfamily *Diaspinae* and also of the genus *Lecanium* have frequently been sent to me in the egg stage and in a great many cases, sometimes many weeks after they were received, these eggs hatched, often in great numbers, and the young larvae were seen crawling about over my desk. Mature viviparous females sometimes give birth to young even after the detached twigs to which they are clinging have begun to wither and die. There is therefore great danger that injurious scale insects may be introduced into new localities through the medium of the mails.

EXPLANTION OF TERMS.

ANUS.—The terminal opening of the alimentary canal. A more or less circular orifice on the dorsal surface of the pygidium. It varies in location from a point near the margin of the pygidium to one anterior of the groups of circumgenital gland-orifices. See Plate 4, Fig. 5 P.

CARINA (plural carinae).—An elevated ridge running longitudinally on the dorsal surface of the male scales of certain genera. Carinae also sometimes occur on female scales.

CARINATE.—Having carinae. For a description see Carina.

CIRCUMGENITAL GLAND-ORIFICES.—These are circular gland-orifices arranged in groups around the genital aperture and furnish a powdery secretion for dusting over the eggs as they issue from the body. See Plate 4, Fig. 5 A.

DORSAL GLAND-ORIFICES.—On the dorsal surface of the pygidium are oval orifices through which the glandular secretions of which the scale is formed, arè discharged. These are arranged in more or less distinct rows which mark the dividing lines of the transformed segments. Each row is usually divided near the middle forming two groups which are termed the anterior and posterior groups. These are shown at B and C, Plate 4, Fig. 5. These rows are designated as first, second, third and fourth; the first row being the one nearest the median line of the body and always extending to the edge of the pygidium between the median and second pair of lobes. See Plate 4, Fig. 5. In a very few species of the *Diaspinae* another poorly defined row occurs still nearer the median line and extends to the edge of the pygidium between the median lobes.

EXUVIA (plural exuviae).—The dorsal integument of the early stages which has been molted off and incorporated into the scale. The smallest and uppermost exuvia is designated as the *first* and the larger under one as the *second*.

FIRST EXUVIA.—See Exuvia.

GLAND-BEARING PROMINENCE.—A prominence on the margin of the pygidium bearing a gland-opening on the dorsal surface. See Plate 4, Fig. 5 J.

GLAND-ORIFICE.—The external opening through which a gland pours its secretions.

GLAND-SPINES.—Spiny appendages each of which is supplied with a single gland whose orifice is at the tip. Other authors have called all appendages of this nature " plates," " squames," " scaly hairs," without distinguishing between the fimbricated appendages of *Aspidiotus*, *Parlatoria* and certain other genera (Plate 4, Figs. 3 and 4) which are not supplied with glands and the spine-like appendages here described. Gland-spines are shown on Plate 4, Fig. 5 H, and also on Plate 6, Figs. 5 and 10. For the sake of brevity a formula has been adopted in giving the number of the gland-spines on the pygidium. Thus in the description of *Chionaspis salicis*, the formula for the gland-spines is given as 1, 1-2, 1-2, 1-2, 3-7, which means that the first group outside of the median lobes contains one, the second, third and fourth one or two each, and the fifth from three to seven.

LOBES.—When lobes are present in the *Diaspinae* they occur at the extremity of the body and are in pairs, there being one pair to each of the transformed segments. Where one pair is present it occurs on segment twelve ; where two pairs are present, on segments eleven, twelve etc., each additional pair being placed on the next anterior unoccupied segment. The terminal pair (Plate 4, Fig. 5 K) is designated as the first or median pair. The others are designated as second, third and fourth pair, etc., according to their position as second, third and fourth from the median pair. See Plate 4, Fig. 5. In the two genera of this paper the second and third pairs, which are the only ones that occur beside the median pair, each lobe is composed of two distinct *lobules*. See Plate 4, Fig. 5 L and M.

LOBULE.—See lobes.

MARGINAL GLAND-ORIFICE.—On the margin of the pygidium are other gland-orifices precisely like the dorsal gland-orifices except for position. These are designated as the marginal gland-orifices and there are two to each of the transformed segments except near the median line where they are less numerous and more variable. These are represented on Plate 4, Fig. 5 E. It will be seen that part are directly on the margin and part are a little back from the edge.

MEDIAN NOTCH.—A notch in the edge of the pygidium at the posterior extremity of the body. This is a very important characteristic of *Aulacaspis* and *Phenacaspis*. Shown on Plate 4, Fig. 1.

PYGIDIUM.—The pygidium is composed of several of the terminal segments of the body which have been transformed and which together form a flattened organ used as a trowel. No definite dividing line between the pygidium and the rest of the body can be designated, but for the purposes of this paper it is considered to extend to the notch just anterior to the fifth group of gland-spines, counting from the median lobes. Fig. 4, on Plate 5, is a more or less diagramatic representation of the body of a female insect in this group. The pygidium which extends as far anteriorly as the notch between segments seven and eight is seen to be made up of parts quite similar to the segments of the rest of the body.

SCALE.—The entire shield-like covering of a scale insect, composed in part of secreted matter produced by the insect and in part of exuviae molted from the body and incorporated into it.

SECOND EXUVIA.—See exuvia.

SPINES.—Two spines occur on each side of each of the segments of the pygidium, the one above usually being the larger. These are generally considerably smaller than the gland-spines and have a circle at their base. See Plate 4, Fig. 5 F and G.

STYLE.—A long spine-like appendage at the end of the body of the male Coccid.

Genus CHIONASPIS.

Chionaspis Signoret, Ann. Soc. Ent. Fr., Ser. 4, Vol. IX., p. 442 (1869).

Chionaspis Comstock, Ann. Rep. U. S. Dept. Agr., 1880, p. 313(1881).

Chionaspis Comstock, Sec. Ann. Rep. Dept. Ent. Cornell Univ. Expt. Sta., p. 97 (1883).

Chionaspis Douglas, Ent. Mo. Mag., Vol. XXII., p. 245 (1885).

Chionaspis Maskell, Ins. Nox. to Agr. and Plants in New Zealand, p. 54 (1887).

Chionaspis Morgan, Ent. Mo. Mag., Vol. XXV., p. 47 (1888).

Chionaspis Cockerell, Bull. Bot. Dept. Jam., No. 40, p. 9 (1893).

Chionaspis Maskell, Tr. N. Z. Inst., Vol. XXVII., p. 9 (1894).

Chionaspis Green, Coccidae of Ceylon, Pt. I., p. 23 (1896).

Chionaspis Berlese and Leonardi, Riv. di. Pat. Veg., Vol. VI., p. 290 (1898).

SCALE OF FEMALE.—Elongated, nearly parallel-sided or plainly broadened posteriorly; more or less convex. Ventral scale developed only at the anterior end. Exuviae at the anterior extremity, the first one naked and lying partly on the second which is more or less covered by secreted matter. Secreted portion of scale white; exuviae varying from colorless to orange-yellow or brownish.

FEMALE.—Plate 2, Fig. 8. Elongated, broadened posteriorly, distinctly segmented. A more or less distinct group of small nearly circular gland-orifices on each side of each of the abdominal segments (Plate 5, Fig. 8). These are much more distinct just in front of the pygidium than near the anterior extremity of the body. More or less distinct rows of oval gland-orifices on the dorsal surface between the posterior segments (Plate 5, Fig. 8). A group of gland-spines on each side of each of the abdominal segments, more distinct near the pygidium than anteriorly (Plate 5, Fig. 8).

The characters of the pygidium (Plate 5, Fig. 8) are as follows. Two or three pairs of *lobes* present. Median lobes more or less semicircular in outline, their bases either close to each other or touching for more or less of their length, serrate, notched or entire.

Each lobe of the second and third pair composed of two lobules of which the inner one is larger than the outer. Second pair always smaller than the first; third pair always smaller than the second. Gland-spines usually simple though sometimes forked at their tips and usually shortest near the median lobes, gradually increasing in size toward the anterior part of the pygidium.

The spines are usually plainly visible ; those on the dorsal larger than those on the ventral surface. First row of *dorsal gland-orifices* absent; second row usually represented by the anterior group only, though in one species (*dysoxyli*) the posterior group only is present; third and fourth rows always present.

Circumgenital gland-orifices always present and arranged in five groups.

SCALE OF MALE.—Elongated ; tricarinate, unicarinate or without carinae. Ventral scale complete, forming with the upper part a complete tube. Plate 2, Fig. 8 A represents the male scale of *salicis*, the type of this genus. Plate 5, Fig. 1 shows it in cross sections.

REMARKS.

Of the fifteen species and one variety now known in the genus Chionaspis, eleven are from America and one each from Europe, Japan, New Zealand, Ceylon and South Africa. Most of the species are rather northern in their range of distribution, and as a rule occur on the bark of the host plant.

Some of the species are very closely related and it has been only by careful study of a very large amount of material that I have been able to find trustworthy characters by means of which they can be separated. It is my opinion that the true European *salicis* has not been discovered in America and that what Prof. Comstock believed to be this species is distinct, though closely related to it. After a careful study of a mass of material from all parts of this country, I have come to the conclusion that Prof. Comstock's *salicis* is identical with the species described by Walsh as *salicis-nigrae* and it seemed proper to adopt his name, even though his type is lost and no comparison with it can now be made.

I have adopted *salicis* L. as the type of the genus *Chionaspis* for the reason that in his original description of the genus, Signoret mentioned this species as an example, though he did not state definitely that he had taken it as the type; and because the first species he discussed under the genus was *aceris* which I have found to be a synonym of *salicis*.

SYNOPTIC TABLE OF SPECIES.

1. { Median carina of male scale fairly distinct, . . 2.
{ Median carina of male scale very indistinct or absent, 11.

2. { Inner edges of median lobes fused together, See Plate 8, Fig. 3.
{ *americana*.
{ Inner edges of median lobes not fused together, . 3.

3. { Anterior group of second row of dorsal gland-orifices present, 4.
{ Anterior group of second row of dorsal gland-orifices absent,
{ *dysoxyli*.

4. { Inner lobule of the second lobe approximately one-third as
{ wide as the median lobe, ... *wistariae*.
{ Inner lobule of second lobe at least one-half as wide as the
{ median lobe, ... 5.

5. { Mature female scale usually more than 2 mm. long, . 6.
{ Mature female scale usually less than 2 mm. long, . *corni*.

6. { Fifth group of gland-spines numbering from one to three, 9.
{ Fifth group of gland-spines numbering from three to eleven, 7.

7. { Median lobes very broadly rounded at their extremities and set
{ close together. See Plate 5, Fig. 3 and Plate 8, Fig. 6, *furfura*.
{ Median lobes not as above described, . . . 8.

8. { Median lobes indistinctly pointed. See Plate 7, Fig. 9, *lintneri*.
{ Median lobes rounded, . *herbae, salicis, salicis-nigrae*.

9. { Median lobes parallel in general direction, . *pinifoliae*.
{ Median lobes divergent, ... 10.

10. { Median lobes large and prominent. See Plate 8, Fig. 9, *stanotophri*.
{ Median lobes rather small and inconspicuous. See Plate 7,
{ Fig. 4, ... *pinifoliae heterophyllae*.

11. { Inner edges of median lobes fused together. See Plate 8,
{ Fig. 5, ... *caryae*.
{ Inner edges of median lobes free, ... 12

12. { Median lobes parallel in general direction; indistinctly
{ serrate 13
{ Median lobes divergent; distinctly serrate, . . *platani*.

13. { Fifth group of gland-spines numbering less than four, *longiloba*.
{ Fifth group of gland-spines numbering more than four,
{ *ortholobis*.

CHIONASPIS SALICIS.

Coccus salicis Linnaeus, Syst. Nat., Ed. X., Vol. I., p. 456 (1758).

Coccus salicis Linnaeus, Fauna Suec., Ed. II., p. 265 (1761).

Coccus salicis Linnaeus, Syst. Nat., Ed. XII., Vol. I., p. 741 (1766).

Coccus salicis Mueller, Fauna Fred., p. 31 (1767).

Coccus salicis Modeer, Act. Goth., Vol. I., p. 21 (1778).

Coccus salicis Gmelin, Syst. Nat., 2218 (1788).

Coccus salicis De Villers, Syst. Nat., Ed. X., p. 560 (1789).

Coccus salicis Olivier, Encycl. Meth., Vol. VI., p. 96 (1791).

Coccus salicis Schrank, Fauna Boica, Vol. II., Pt. 1, p. 143 (1804).

Coccus saliceti Ratzeburg, Forst-ins., Vol. III., p. 195 (1844).

Aspidiotus salicis Bouché, Stett. Ent. Zeit., Vol. V., p. 294 (1844).

Aspidiotus salicifex Amyot, Monom., p. 480 (1847).

Coccus salicis Macquart, Ann. Soc. Ent. Fr., Vol. XXV. (1847).

Aspidiotus minimus Baerensprung, Zeit. fur Zool. Zoot., p. 168 (1849).

Coccus salicis Macquart,Ann. Soc.Ent.Fr.,2nd Ser.Vol.VII., p.47(1849).

Aspidiotus vaccinii Bouché, Stett. Ent. Zeit., Vol. XII., p. 111 (1851).

Aspidiotus salicis Bouché, Ent. Zeit. Stett., XII., 110 (1851).

Aspidiotus populi Bouché, Stett. Ent. Zeit., Vol. XII., p. 111 (1851).

Aspidiotus saliceti Bouché, Stett. Ent. Zeit., Vol. XII., p. 111 (1851).

Chionaspis populi Signoret, Ann. Soc. Ent. Fr., 4th Ser. Vol. IX., p. 446 (1869).

Chionaspis salicis Signoret, Ann. Soc. Ent. Fr., 4th Ser. Vol. IX., p. 447 (1869).

Chionaspis alni Signoret, Ann. Soc. Ent. Fr., 4th Ser. Vol. IX., p. 443 (1869).

Chionaspis fraxini Signoret, Ann. Soc. Ent. Fr., 4th Ser. Vol. IX., p. 445 (1869).

Chionaspis vaccinii Signoret, Ann. Soc. Ent. Fr., 4th Ser. Vol. IX., p. 448 (1869).

Chionaspis aceris Signoret, Ann. Soc. Ent. Fr., 4th Ser. Vol. IX., p. 442 (1869).

Aspidiotus saliceti Kaltenbach, Pflanzenfeinde aus der Klasse Insekten, p. 587 (1874).

Chionaspis fraxini Ormerod, Man. Inj. Ins., (First Ed.), p. 176 (1881).

Chionaspis salicis F. Löw, Wien. Ent. Zeit., Vol. II., p. 6 (1883).

Chionaspis salicis Targioni-Tozzetti, Annali d'Agricoltura, p. 384 (1884).

Chionaspis vaccinii Goethe, Beobachtung über Schildläuse und deren
  Feinde, angestellt an Obstbaumen und Reben ims
  Rheingau, p. 116 (1884).

Chionaspis fraxini Douglas, Ent. Mon. Mag., Vol. XXII., p.
  • 160 (1885).

Chionaspis populi Douglas, Ent. Mon. Mag., Vol. XXII., p.247 (1885).

Chionaspis salicis Douglas, Ent. Mon. Mag., Vol. XXII., p. 249 (1885).

Chionaspis alni Douglas. Ent. Mon. Mag., Vol. XXII., p. 249 (1885).

Chionaspis aceris Douglas, Ent. Mon. Mag., Vol. XXII., p.159 (1885).

Chionaspis vaccinii Douglas, Ent. Mon. Mag., Vol. XXII., p. 246 (1885).

Chionaspis fraxini Newstead, Ent. Mon. Mag., Vol. XXVI., p.
  436 (1889).

Chionaspis fraxini Mosley, Naturalists' Guide, Vol. VI., p. 8 (1890).

Chionaspis populi Mosley, Naturalists' Guide, Vol. VI., p. 31 (1890).

Chionaspis fraxini Curtis, Manifestation of Disease in Forest Trees,
  p. 33 (1892).

Chionaspis salicis Morgan, Ent. Mon. Mag., Vol. XXIX., p. 16 (1892).

Chionaspis salicis Lintner, Ninth Rep. Ins. N. Y., p. 411 (1893).

Chionaspis fraxini ———, Brit. Nat., p. 23 (1894).

Aspidiotus fraxini Henschel, Die schadlichen Forst-und Obstbaum-
  Insekten, p. 514 (1895).

Aspidiotus salicis Henschel, Die schadlichen Forst-und Obstbaum-
  Insekten, p. 514 (1895).

Chionaspis salicis Gillette and Baker, Hemipt. of Colo., p.129 (1895).

Chionaspis alni Cockerell, Can. Ent., Vol. XXVII., p. 33 (1895).

Chionaspis salicis Reuter, Meddel. Soc. Fauna Flo. Fenn., Hft. 22, p.
  21 (1896).

Chionaspis vaccinii Cockerell, Bull. U. S. Dept. Agr., Div. Ent., Tech.
  Ser., No. 4, p. 54 (1896).

Chionaspis salicis Douglas, Note on Some British Coccidae, (No. 2), p. 249 (1896).

Aspidiotus salicis Eckstein, Forstliche Zoologie, p. 558 (1897).

Chionaspis salicis Berlese and Leonardi, Chermotheca Italica, III., Nos. 55, 56 and 57.

EGG.—Slightly more than .2 mm. long; ellipsoidal, reddish-purple. Miss Ormerod states that the color of the eggs is crimson, but it seems probable that the specimens she had for examination were about to hatch in which case they would be more reddish in color than those in which the embryos had not developed. I have seen only newly laid specimens.

SCALE OF FEMALE.—Plate 2, Fig. 8. Length, 2.2—2.8 mm. Decidedly broadened posteriorly ; moderately strong in texture ; snow white or dirty white in color. Exuviae .8—.9 mm. long ; varying in color from orange-yellow to brown or sometimes almost colorless.

FEMALE.—According to Signoret the color of the body (Plate 5, Fig. 8), is reddish-yellow. Median *lobes* (Plate 7, Fig. 1) about as broad as long, obscurely striate, with edges somewhat triangular, sometimes faintly serrate on the sides. Second and third lobes each with the inner lobule much larger than the outer ; striate, sometimes obscurely serrate on the outer edge. The *gland-spines* are arranged as follows : 1, 1-2, 1-2, 1-2, 3-7. The first one small, though readily seen. When two occur together one is smaller and often directly above the other. Second row of *dorsal gland-orifices* represented only by the anterior group consisting of 2—6 orifices. Third row with 4—9 orifices in the anterior and 5—9 in the posterior group. Fourth row with 3—8 orifices in the anterior and 3—9 in the posterior group.* Median group of *circumgenital gland-orifices*, 11—17 ; anterior laterals, 26—44 : posterior laterals, 18—29.

SCALE OF MALE.—Plate 2, Fig. 8 A. Length, .7—1 mm. Of definite outline, distinctly carinated. Exuvia pale yellow or colorless, occupying one-third to one-half the length of the scale.

MALE.†—Elongated, flattened, red or sometimes yellowish ; apterous or with wings. Antennae with third joint longest, fourth, fifth,

---

*Occasionally there are a few scattering *gland-orifices* precisely like those around the genital opening. These represent the second arch which has been the distinguishing character of the genus *Poliaspis*. This genus is no longer retained.

†The description of the male is compiled from the writings of Bouché, Signoret and Newstead. I have never seen specimens of this sex.

sixth, seventh and ninth joints of equal length; eighth joint shortest and a little thickened. Prothorax bearing a small protuberance on each side in front under the eye. Wings when present, whitish. Style about as long as the body.

REMARKS.

So far as known *C. salicis* is confined to Europe. It has been recorded by Douglas in England, by Reuter in Finland and by Signoret in Vienna, Austria and also in Switzerland. Although Signoret does not state definitely that it occurs in France we would infer that it is found there from the fact that he gives an account of it in his " Essai sur les Cochenilles " without giving a locality. The Department of Agriculture contains specimens also from Bohemia and Hamburg, Germany and the species has been sent me from Italy by Mr. Karl L. Kafka.

The species has been recorded by various authors on the following plants: *Salix hermaphrodita, S. alba, S. viminalis, S. holoserica, Fraxinus excelsior, Sarcothamnus scoparius, Populus nigra, P. Pyramidalis, Vaccinium myrtillus and Alnus communis.* Willow, ash, maple, poplar and alder have also been given without mentioning the species. The Department of Agriculture contains specimens from Dr. E. Reuter on *Vaccinium vitis-idaea* and from Dr. L. Rey of Hamburg on *Tilia parvifolia.* Mr. Karl L. Kafka of Vienna has sent me specimens on *Alnus glutinosa, Populus tremuloides, Sarcothamnus vulgare, Cornus sanguinea* and *Acer pseudoplatanus.*

The following scattering statements from various authors indicate briefly the life history of the species. Ratzeburg states that there is only one generation. Bouché has found that " 20—30 reddish purple eggs " are laid in the fall and hatch during the first warm days of the spring. He observed that they hatch as early as February and March. Signoret states that he has found the males in the pupal stage in the month of August. Newstead, however, bred a large number of males in the last week of July and the first week of August. This difference in time of development of the male is doubtless due to difference in localilty. According to Bouché the length of the pupal stage is from eight to fourteen days.

In the writings of Bouché and Ratzeburg it is stated that the male is apterous, while Signoret affirms that it is winged, and not until the year 1889 was the apparent discrepancy cleared up. In the Entomologist's Monthly Magazine for 1889, Newstead states that he bred quantities of males which were about evenly divided between winged and apterous individuals. In recent years we have learned that it is not an uncommon occurrence for males to be both winged and apterous in the same species.

This species is found only on the bark of its host-plants. On ash it confines its attack to the young and tender growth, avoiding the trunk and larger limbs. It often becomes so abundant as to cause injury to the tree.

In the preparation of the description of this species I have had a very large amount of material for examination, from a wide range of localities in Europe. The specimens were sent me under the old specific names of *populi*, *alni*, *fraxini*, *vaccinii* and *aceris* as well as *salicis*. A series of slides has been made from each lot of specimens received and an examination of these slides, as well as of the scales, *in situ* on the bark has led me to believe them all to belong to the same species, and as *salicis* has priority over the other names, it has been retained. Other authors have believed *fraxini* to be only a synonym of *salicis* and Signoret doubted if *populi* was a valid species. Reuter in 1896 placed *vaccinii* also as a synonym of *salicis*. In his original description of *aceris*, Signoret states that the eggs are of a greenish color, while in *salicis* they are known to be reddish purple. In all species of the genus as far as they have been described, or as far as I have observed them, the eggs are alike in color and in no case have I known of their having any greenish tinge. Moreover dead and shrivelled eggs of *aceris* are of precisely the same color as eggs of *salicis* in the same condition. I am therefore led to think that Signoret was mistaken and have placed *aceris* also as a synonym of *salicis* as there are no structural characters by which to separate them.

No enemies of this species have been recorded.

CHIONASPIS CORNI n. sp.

SCALE OF FEMALE.—Plate 2, Fig. 1. Length, 1.6—2 mm. Distinctly broadened posteriorly, rather thin, white. Exuviae .7 mm., the first one lying almost entirely on the second ; bright orange-yellow or slightly brown in color.

FEMALE.—Plate 8, Fig. 8. Median *lobes* entire or serrate, rather short and broad, sometimes obscurely pointed. Second and third pairs sometimes very small; inner lobule larger than the outer. *Gland-spines* rather long and slender, arranged as follows : 1, 1, 1-2, 1-2, 4-6. Second row of *dorsal gland-orifices* represented by the anterior group consisting of 2—5 orifices. Third row with 4—5 orifices in the anterior and 5—7 in the posterior group. Fourth row with 4—7 orifices in the anterior and 6—9 in the posterior group. Median group of *circumgenital gland-orifices*, 9—15 ; anterior laterals, 17—28 ; posterior laterals, 9—17.

SCALE OF MALE.—Plate 2, Fig. 1 A. Length, .6—.8 mm., moderately but plainly tri-carinate. Exuvia pale yellow occupying one-third to one-half the length of the scale.

REMARKS.

My attention was first called to this insect by Mr. A. H. Kirkland who sent me specimens from Reading, Mass. on *Cornus paniculata* and *C. alternifolia*. The Department of Agriculture contains specimens on *Cornus paniculata*. The occurrence of the species in Reading was in a nursery where a block of dogwood shrubs was quite badly infested, some plants almost entirely covered near the base.

CHIONASPIS LONGILOBA n. sp.

SCALE OF FEMALE.—Plate 2, Fig. 2. Length 1.5—2 mm. Moderately strong in texture, dirty white in color. Exuviae, 8 mm. long, dull yellowish brown.

FEMALE.—Plate 8, Fig. 7. Median *lobes* well developed and conspicuous ; obscurely pointed, serrate. Second and third pairs with the inner lobule larger than the outer ; serrate. Inner lobule of the second lobe long and conspicuous. The lobes of this species are

• perceptibly longer than in any other of the group. The *gland-spines* are arranged as follows : 1, 2, 1-2, 1-2, 2-3. Those on the anterior part of the pygidium are large and conspicuous, decreasing in size toward the median lobes. Second row of *dorsal gland-orifices* represented by the anterior group consisting of 4—5 orifices. Third row with 5—7 orifices in the anterior and 4—5 in the posterior group. Fourth row with 5—6 orifices in the anterior and 5—7 in the posterior group. Median group of *circumgenital gland-orifices* 10—16 ; anterior laterals, 20—24 ; posterior laterals, 10—17.

SCALE OF MALE.—Plate 2, Fig. 2 A. Length, .6—.8 mm. Oval, without carinae. Exuvia brownish or colorless.

REMARKS.

The absence of carinae on the male scales of this insect and *C. ortholobis* indicates a relationship between the two species and separates them from all others of the genus. *C. longiloba* can be separated from *C. ortholobis* by the smaller size of the scales and the greater length and more pointed form of the median lobes in *C. longiloba*.

The specimens from which the foregoing descriptions were made are from the Department of Agriculture and were collected on cottonwood in Texas.

CHIONASPIS ORTHOLOBIS.

Chionaspis ortholobis Comstock, Rep. U. S. Dept. Agr., 1880, p. 317 (1881).

Chionaspis ortholobis Comstock, Second Rep. Dept. of Ent. Cornell Univ. Expt. Sta., p. 105 (1883).

Chionaspis ortholobis Packard, Fifth Rep. U.S. Ent. Com., p. 594(1890).

Chionaspis ortholobis Cockerell, Can. Ent., Vol. XXVI., p. 189 (1894).

Chionaspis ortholobis Howard, Ins. Life, Vol. VI., p. 328 (1894).

Chionaspis ortholobis Gillette & Baker, Hemipt. of Colo., p. 129 (1895).

Chionaspis ortholobis Cockerell, Bull. 24, N. Mex. Ag'l. Expt. Sta., p. 38 (1897).

Chionaspis ortholobis Osborn, Contr. from Dept. of Zoöl. and Ent. Ia. Ag'l. College, No. 3. p. 5 (1898).

2

EGG.—Prof. Comstock states that the eggs are dark purple in color.

SCALE OF FEMALE.—Plate 3, Fig. 8. Length, 2—2.5 mm. Moderately elongated, broadest near the middle of the scale; dirty white. Exuviae .8mm. long, brown.

FEMALE.—Plate 8, Fig. 2. Median lobes straight and parallel, having the appearance of being set closely together; rounded on their extremities, sometimes obscurely serrate on the sides. Second and third pairs with the inner lobule larger than the outer, a little oblique; entire or obscurely serrate. The *gland-spines* are arranged as follows: 1, 1-2, 1-2, 2, 4-5. The first one is small and blunt, and they are all as a rule noticeably smaller than in *lintneri* or *salicis-nigrae*. Second row of *dorsal gland-orifices* represented by the anterior group consisting of 4—7 orifices. Third row with 7—9 orifices in the anterior and 5—8 in the posterior group. Fourth row with 10—11 orifices in the anterior and 5—9 in the posterior group. Median group of *circumgenital gland-orifices*, 10—25; anterior laterals, 18—35; posterior laterals, 16—24.

SCALE OF MALE.—Plate 3, Fig. 8A. Length, .6—.8 mm. Oval, without carinae; exuvia pale brown or almost colorless.

REMARKS.

This species was first described from Southern California and has since been frequently found in that state. The Department of Agriculture contains specimens from Hartington, Neb., and Missouri. I have already received examples from Riley Co., Kansas from Mr. P. J. Parrott. Prof. Comstock's specimens were found on willow where they infested chiefly the young whip-like shoots arising from the trunks of the trees. Specimens from the Department of Agriculture and from Mr. P. J. Parrott were taken from cottonwood. Prof. Comstock found eggs of this species under the scales on September 12. This would indicate that the insect passes the winter in the egg stage as do its near relatives in this country and Europe.

In the preparation of the foregoing descriptions I have had cotypes for examination as well as many hundreds of other specimens.

CHIONASPIS SALICIS-NIGRAE.

Aspidiotus salicis-nigrae Walsh, First Rep. Nox. Ins. Ill., p. 39 (1867).

Mytilaspis salicis Le Baron, Trans. Ill. Hort. Soc., app. p. 140 (1871).

Mytilaspis salicis Le Baron, Second Rep. St. Ent. Ill., p. 140 (1872).

Chionaspis salicis Comstock, Rep. U. S. Dept. Agr., 1880, p. 320 (1881).

Chionaspis salicis Osborn, Trans. Ia. St. Hort. Soc., Vol. XVII., p. 214 (1882).

Chionaspis salicis Comstock, Second Rep. Dept. Ent. Cornell Univ. Expt. Sta., p. 106 (1883).

Chionaspis salicis Comstock, Intro. Ent., Part I, p. 151 (1888).

Chionaspis salicis Packard, Fifth Rep. U. S. Ent. Com., p. 593 (1890).

Mytilaspis salicis Forbes, Seventeenth Rep. Nox. and Benif. Ins. Ill., app. p. 23 (1891).

Chionaspis salicis Lugger, Bull. 43, Minn. Ag'l. Expt. Sta., p. 224 (1895).

Chionaspis salicis Lugger, First Ann. Rep. Ent. Minn., p. 128 (1895).

Chionaspis salicis Osborn, Proc. Ia. Acad. Sci., Vol. V., p. 224 (1898).

Chionaspis salicis Osborn, Contr. from Dept. of Zoöl. and Ent. Ia. Ag'l. Coll., No. 3, p. 4 (1898).

Chionaspis ortholobis Bruneri Cockerell, Can. Ent., Vol. XXX., p. 135 (1898).

EGG.—Oval, reddish-purple in color.

SCALE OF FEMALE.—Plate 3, Fig. 1. Length, 2.6—4 mm.: moderately elongated, broadest near the middle, distinctly convex, white. Exuviae .8—.9 mm. long, usually yellowish-brown but sometimes almost colorless.

FEMALE.—Pygidium usually very broad in proportion to its length. Median *lobes* (Plate 7, Fig. 3,) broad, short, rounded, entire or faintly serrate. Second and third pairs with the inner lobule larger than the outer, entire or faintly serrate. Third pair often almost obsolete. The *gland-spines* are arranged as follows: 1, 1-2, 1-2, 1-3, 5-6. The *dorsal gland-orifices* are often of two kinds in this species. Beside the usual groups of oval orifices there frequently occur smaller circular ones which are also placed in groups. In such examples the anterior group of oval orifices is wholly or in part replaced by one of these groups, and anterior to each of the inner groups of oval orifices on the pygidium and abdominal segments is another group of circular orifices. Some specimens have the anterior group of the second row made up of both circular and oval orifices. The oval orifices are arranged as follows : third row with 6—9 orifices in the anterior and 5—8 in the posterior group ; fourth row with 8—10 orifices in the anterior and 8—11 in the posterior group. Median group of *circumgenital gland-orifices*, 21—36 ; anterior laterals, 31—45 ; posterior laterals, 28—32.

SCALE OF MALE.—Plate 3, Fig. 1A. Length, 1—1.2 mm. Parallel-sided or slightly broadened posteriorly, with the posterior extremity rounded; distinctly but feebly tri-carinated. Exuvia brown or almost colorless, occupying about one-third the length of the scale.

REMARKS.

The nearest relative of *C. salicis-nigrae* in America is *C. lintneri*, but the two species may be readily distinguished by the fact that in *C. salicis-nigrae* the median lobes are rounded while in *C. lintneri* they are obscurely pointed. *C. corni* may be readily distinguished by the smaller size, the female scale never reaching the minimum size of *C. salicis-nigrae*. *C. ortholobis* and *C. longiloba* are readily separated by the fact that the male scales in these two species are without carinae.

C. salicis-nigrae is undoubtedly a native of this country where it has a very wide distribution. It has been sent to me more frequently than any other species treated of in this paper. Prof. Comstock has recorded it at Ithaca, N. Y., and St. Louis, Mo., Prof. Osborn at Ames and Davenport, Ia., and Prof. Cockerell in Nebraska. The Department of Agriculture contains specimens from Mankato, Kansas; Las Cruces, N. M.; Lincoln, Neb.; Norman, Neb.; Lafayette, Ind.; Champaign, Ill.; St. Anthony Park, Minn.; New York; West Cliff, Colo.; Pullman, Wash.; Arizona ; Siskiyou Co., Cal. The species has also been sent me from the following localities : Paraje, N. Mex., (Cockerell); Huntington, Mass.: Bedford, Mass.; Lobster Lake, Me., (Kirkland); Malden, Mass. (Burgess); Lawrence, Mass. (King); Riley Co., Kan. (Parrott); Cobden, Ill., and Kappa, Ill. (Forbes); Madeira Co., Cal. (Craw); Pullman, Wash., (Piper); Leaming, Kingston and Kingsville, Ont., Canada (Fletcher).

This species is often very abundant, sometimes completely covering the bark of the host-plant. Reports of trees having been killed by this insect are not infrequent. Various authors have given willow and cottonwood as food-plants of ·C. *salicis-nigrae* and Prof. Osborn has taken it on poplar. In the Department of Agriculture are examples on *Salix alba*, *S. nigra*, *S. alba* var. *camellia*, *Cornus pubescens*, *C. asperifolia*, Balm of Gilead and Russian poplar. In addition to these I have received specimens on *Liriodendron tulipifera* from Dr. James Fletcher, *Cornus stolonifera* and *C. sericea* from Mr. A. H. Kirkland, *Ceanothus* from Mr. Alex. Craw and on *Amelanchier canadensis* from Mr. G. B. King.

This species passes the winter in the egg stage, about seventy-five eggs occurring under each scale, according to LeBaron. The same author observed the " deep-red " young larvae hatching on May 8. Professor Lugger has seen the eggs hatching about the first of June, but the difference in time is probably due to difference in locality or variation in season. There is no published statement of the number of broods of this insect and I have never had an opportunity of studying its habits. We are entirely without information, also, as to the appearance of the male insect.

A few remarks on the names given to this insect seem desirable and will explain my reasons for retaining the name *salicis-nigrae*. Professor Comstock was the first to consider our species identical with the European *salicis*, but his conclusions were based on only two lots of specimens from this country. Had his series been more extended his conclusions probably would have been different. Several years before, LeBaron described the insect as new under the name of *Mytilaspis salicis*, apparently unaware of the fact that this specific name was preoccupied. Early in my studies on this genus it became evident that the true European *salicis* had not been discovered in this country, and that it was necessary to give a name to our American insect. It must be admitted that Walsh's description is very incomplete and applies equally well to several other allied species, but, as far as I know, this is the only species in the group which occurs in Illinois, the state from which Walsh described his species, with the exception of *corni* which is smaller and confined to *Cornus*. Walsh's type of the species is lost, probably having been burned with the rest of his collection in the great Chicago fire. The only other species now known from which Walsh's description could

have been made are, *lintneri* which occurs only in the eastern part of
the United States and Canada, *ortholobis* which is a western species
and *longiloba* which is found only in Texas. Specimens of *ortholobis*
have been taken, however, from Missouri and Kansas and this fact
has tended to make the identity of *salicis-nigrae* less certain; yet the
weight of evidence leads to the conclusion that the species now
before me is really identical with that described by Walsh.

CHIONASPIS LINTNERI.

Chionaspis lintneri Comstock, Second Rep. Dept. Ent. Cornell Univ.
Expt. Sta., p. 103 (1883).
Chionaspis Lintneri Cockerell, Can. Ent., Vol. XXVII., p. 33 (1895).
Chionaspis Lintneri betulae Cooley, Can. Ent., Vol. XXX., p. 85 (1898).
Chionaspis Lintneri Cooley, Can. Ent., Vol. XXX., p. 89 (1898).

SCALE OF FEMALE.—Plate 3, Fig. 3. Length, 2.5—3.2 mm.
Decidedly broadened posteriorly, somewhat flattened, usually thin
and flexible; dull dirty white or snow-white in color. Exuviae
1 mm. long, yellowish-brown. In many of the specimens examined
the small anterior exuvia had been brushed off and lost; scarcely a
specimen among the cotypes of the species which I have seen has
this exuvia present. The second exuvia is .8 mm. long.

FEMALE.—Plate 7, Fig. 9. Median *lobes* obscurely pointed and
faintly serrate. Second and third pairs with the inner lobule larger
than the outer; faintly serrate. The *gland-spines* are long and slender and are arranged as follows: 1, 1-2, 2, 1-3, 6-9. Second
row of *dorsal gland-orifices* represented by the anterior group consisting of 3—6 orifices. Third row with 4—6 orifices in the anterior
and 5—7 in the posterior group. Fourth row with 6—8 orifices in
the anterior and 8—10 in the posterior group. Median group of
circumgenital gland-orifices, 11—19; anterior laterals, 25—42; posterior laterals, 19—28.

SCALE OF MALE.—Plate 3, Fig. 3 A. Length, .8—1 mm. Parallel-sided, distinctly tri-carinate. Exuvia yellow or almost colorless,
occupying about two-fifths of the length of the scale.

23

REMARKS.

C. lintneri is a native North American insect and has been taken only in the eastern United States and eastern Canada. In the original description of this insect Professor Comstock stated that he had received his specimens from the State Entomologist of New York, and though it is not stated where the specimens were collected, we may infer that they came from New York state. Prof. Cockerell has recorded the species from Charlottetown, Prince Edward Island. The Department of Agriculture contains examples from Chateaugay, Quebec, Canada; Ithaca, N. Y. and "opposite Alexandria," D. C. Two lots of specimens of doubtful locality but probably from Ottawa, Can. and Buffalo, N. Y. were received from Prof. Cockerell and I have also received examples from Stoneham, Mass. from Mr. Kirkland and from Ballardvale, Andover and Methuen, Mass. from Mr. G. B. King.

The food plants of the species already published are "Alder," *Viburnum lantanoides*, and *Betula papyrifera*. The Department of Agriculture contains specimens found on *Cornus stolaniger* and *Salix* sp. and it has been sent to me on *Lindera odorifera* and *Corylus americana* by Mr. G. B. King, and on *Alnus serrulata* by Mr. A. H. Kirkland. It occurs also on *Cornus alternifolia* and *C. stolonifera*. A very large percentage of the examples received from Stoneham, Mass. bear evidence of having been parasitized, though no specimens of the parasite have ever been captured.

In the preparation of the descriptions of this insect I have had a part of Prof. Comstock's cotypes for examination.

CHIONASPIS FURFURA.

—— —— Harris, Rep. Ins. of Mass. Inj. Veg., p. 202 (1841).

Aspidiotus furfurus Fitch, Trans. N. Y. St. Ag'l. Soc., Vol. XVI., p. 352 (1856).

Aspidiotus cerasi Fitch, Trans. N. Y. St. Ag'l. Soc., Vol. XVI., p. 368 (1856).

Aspidiotus furfurus Fitch, Third Rep. Nox. and Other Ins., p. 352 (1857).

Aspidiotus cerasi Fitch, Third Rep. Nox. and Other Ins., p.368 (1857).

———— ———— Harris, Treat. Ins. Inj. Veg. (Third Ed.), p. 254 (1862).

Coccus ? Harrisii Walsh, Pract. Ent., Vol. II., p. 31 (1866).

Aspidiotus Harrisii Walsh, Pract. Ent., Vol. II., p. 119 (1867).

Aspidiotus Harrisii Walsh, First Rep. Nox. Ins. Ill., pp. 36, 53(1868).

Aspidiotus Harrisii Riley, First Ann. Rep. Ins. Mo., p. 7 (1869).

Aspidiotus Harrisii Riley, Am. Ent., Vol. II., pp. 110, 181 (1870).

Aspidiotus Harrisii Riley, Second Ann. Rep. Ins. Mo., p. 9 (1870).

Aspidiotus Harrisii Bethune, Rep. Ent. Soc. Ont., I., p. 303 (1870).

Aspidiotus Harrisii Glover, Ann. Rep. U. S. Dept. Agr., 1870, p. 88 (1871).

Aspidiotus Harrisii Bessey, Rep. Ia. St. Ag'l. Soc., 1874, p. 232 (1875).

Diaspis Harrisii Signoret, Ann. Soc. Ent. Fr., Ser. 4, Vol. XVI., p. 604 (1876).

Aspidiotus Harrisii Thomas, Seventh Rep. Ins. Ill., p. 108 (1878).

Chionaspis furfurus Comstock, Ann. Rep. U. S. Dept. Agr., 1880, p. 315 (1881).

Diaspis Harrisii Riley, Am. Nat., Vol. XV., p. 487 (1881).

Chionaspis furfurus Lintner, First Ann. Rep. Inj. Ins. N. Y., p. 331 (1882).

Aspidiotus Harrisii Packard, Guide Study Ins., p. 530 (1883).

Chionaspis furfurus Osborn, Trans. Ia. St. Hort. Soc., Vol. XVII., p. 211 (1883).

Chionaspis furfurus Hagen, Can. Ent., Vol. XVI., p. 161 (1884).

Chionaspis furfurus Osborn, Bull. Ia. Ag'l. Coll. Expt. Sta., No. 2 (1884).

Chionaspis furfurus Comstock, Intro. to Ent., Pt. I., p. 151 (1888).

Chionaspis furfurus Lintner, Fourth Ann. Rep. Inj. Ins. N. Y., p. 208 (1888).

Chionaspis furfurus Tryon, Rep. Ins. and Fung. Pests, No. 1, p. 89 (1889).

Chionaspis furfurus Riley-Howard, Ins. Life, Vol. I., p. 324 (1889).

Chionaspis furfurus Lintner, Fifth Ann. Rep. Inj. Ins. N. Y., pp. 300, 326 (1889).

Aspidiotus cerasi Saunders, Ins. Inj. to Fruits, p. 204 (1889).

" A species of *Coccus* " Downing, Fruits and Fruit Trees of America, p. 66 (1890).

Chionaspis furfurus Riley-Howard, Ins. Life, Vol. III., p. 4 (1890).

Chionaspis furfurus Weed (C. M.), Bull. Ohio Ag'l. Expt. Sta., Vol. III., No. 4, p. 128 (1890).

Chionaspis furfurus Packard, Fifth Rep. U. S. Ent. Com., p. 537 (1890).

Chionaspis furfurus Weed (C. M.), Insects and Insecticides, p. 66 (1891).

Chionaspis furfurus Gillette, Ins. Life, Vol. III., p. 259 (1891).

Chionaspis furfurus Weed (C. M.), Ann. Rep. Colum. Hort. Soc., 1890, p. 16 (1891).

Chionaspis furfurus Troop, Trans. Ind. Hort. Soc., 1891, p. 75 (1892).

Chionaspis furfurus Morgan, Ent. Mo. Mag.,Vol. XXIX., p. 16 (1892).

Chionaspis furfurus Webster, Bull. Ohio Ag'l. Expt. Sta., No. 45, p. 208 (1892).

Chionaspis furfurus Lintner, Eighth Ann. Rep. Inj. Ins. N. Y., pp. 293, 299 (1893).

Chionaspis furfurus Lintner, Ninth Rep. Inj. Ins. N. Y., pp. 440, 464 (1893).

Chionaspis furfurus Osborn, Rep. Ia. St. Hort. Soc.,Vol. XXVII., p. 122 (1893).

Chionaspis furfurus Marlatt, Ins. Life, Vol. VII., p. 120 (1894).

Chionaspis furfurus Smith, Ann. Rep. N. J. Ag'l. Expt. Sta., 1894, p. 496 (1894).

Chionaspis furfurus Bruner, Ann. Rep. Nebr. St. Hort. Soc., 1894, p. 175 (1894).

Chionaspis furfurus Howard, Ins. Life, Vol. VII., p. 5 (1894).

Chionaspis furfurus Smith, Ins. Life, Vol. VII., p. 186 (1894).

Chionaspis furfurus Howard, Can. Ent., Vol. XXVI., p. 354 (1894).

Chionaspis furfurus Howard, Yearbook U. S. Dept. Agr., 1884, p. 259 (1895).

Chionaspis furfurus Lintner, Tenth Ann. Rep. Inj. Ins. N. Y., p. 518 (1895).

Chionaspis furfurus Fletcher, Ann. Rep. Can. Expt. Farm, 1895, p. 148 (1896).

Chionaspis furfurus Howard, Trans. Mass. Hort. Soc., 1896, p. 89 (1896).

Chionaspis furfurus Lintner, Eleventh Ann. Rep. Inj. Ins. N. Y., pp. 202, 271, 288 (1896).

Chionaspis furfurus Garman, Eighth Ann. Rep. Ky. Ag'l. Expt. Sta., p. XXXVII (1896).

Chionaspis furfurus Smith, Econ. Ent., p. 119 (1896).

Chionaspis furfurus Coons, Rep. Sec. Bd. Agr. Conn., 1896, p. 16 (1896).

Chionaspis furfurus Starnes, Bull. Ga. Ag'l. Expt. Sta., No. 36, p. 27 (1897).

Chionaspis furfurus Lowe, Bull. N. Y. Ag'l. Expt. Sta., p. 582 (1897).

Chionaspis furfurus Lintner, Twelfth Ann. Rep. Inj. Ins. N. Y., p. 348 (1897).

Chionaspis furfurus Webster, Bull. Ohio Ag'l. Expt. Sta., No. 81, p. 210 (1897).

Chionaspis furfurus Osborn, Proc. Ia. Acad. Sci., Vol. V., p. 224 (1898).

Chionaspis furfurus Gillette, Bull. Colo. Ag'l. Expt. Sta., No. 47, p. 12 (1898).

Chionaspis furfurus Kirkland, Mass. Crop Rep., June, 1898, p. 28 (1898).

Chionaspis furfurus Pettit, Bull. Mich. Ag'l. Expt. Sta., p. 415 (1898).

Chionaspis furfurus Osborn, Contr. from Dept. Zool. and Ent. Ia. Ag'l. Col., No. 3, p. 4 (1898).

Chionaspis furfurus var. *fulvus* King, Psyche, Vol. VIII., p. 334 (1899).

EGG.—Length, .25 mm. Ellipsoidal in form, reddish-purple in color.

SCALE OF FEMALE.—Plate 2, Fig. 7. Length, 2.3 mm. Decidedly broadened posteriorly, slightly convex, thin but not transparent; dirty white or snow white. Exuviae unusually small in proportion to the secreted part; 1 mm. long; yellowish-brown. The first exuvia is often brushed off leaving only the second which is .7 mm. long.

FEMALE.—Plate 5, Fig. 3 and Plate 8, Fig. 6. Median and second pairs of *lobes* well developed ; third pair rudimentary. Median lobes broad and short, entire, plainly striate ; with oblique thickened bars at their bases. Second pair usually entire, striate ; inner lobule larger than the outer, oblique and with the inner edge thickened. Third pair serrate, striate, usually very short but sometimes fairly well developed. The *gland-spines* are arranged as follows: 1, 1, 1, 1, 4-9. The one nearest the median lobe on each side is very small and blunt, sometimes wanting. Second row of *dorsal gland-orifices* absent. Third row with 2—3 orifices in the anterior and 3—5 in the posterior group. Fourth row with 2—3 orifices in the anterior and 2—4 in the posterior group. Median group of *circumgenital, gland-orifices*, 7—16 ; anterior laterals, 22—32 ; posterior laterals, 16—22.

SCALE OF MALE.—Plate 2, Fig. 7 A. Length, .7—.9 mm. Surface above rather rough in texture ; distinctly tri-carinate. Exuvia pale yellow, occupying about one-third the length of the scale.

MALE.—Professor Comstock has described the male as follows : " Yellow, marked with irregular reddish-brown spots ; thoracic band reddish-brown, sometimes darker than the other markings. Length of body including style, .62 mm. (.02 inch) ; length of style, .18 mm. (.0006 inch). On each side of the anterior part of the thorax there is a black spot which resembles an eye."

I have never seen the male insect.

REMARKS.

Chionaspis furfura is a native of this country but Morgan discovered it in England on *Ribes sanguineum* which had been carried there from America. This is without doubt the best known species of the genus in the United States, occupying the same position in this respect that *salicis* does in Europe. A detailed account of its distribution in this country would be of little use since the fact that the species is not recorded from any particular locality in any infested state is no indication that it does not occur there. A list of the states only is therefore given. It has been recorded by various authors from Massachusetts, New York, New Jersey, Delaware, Pennsylvania, Maryland, Virginia, District of Columbia, Tennessee, Georgia, Kansas, Mississippi, Ohio, Indiana, Illinois, Missouri, Iowa, Nebraska, South Dakota and Southern California. Dr. Fletcher has recorded the species also from Leamington, Ont., Canada.

While nurserymen and orchardists as well as entomologists regard *Chionaspis furfura* of less importance than *Mytilaspis pomorum*, it is admitted to be very destructive at times. Prof. Osborn writing of the insect says: " This species is at times very plentiful and destructive in our orchards and whenever seen should be promptly treated." Dr. Lintner says, " This scale insect, known to science as Chionaspis furfurus (Fitch), is quite common in the state of New York, where, it is believed to be more numerous and more injurious than in any other of the United States. I have recently seen an orchard of the Kieffer pear, in Columbia Co., N. Y., in which the trunks of from three to four inches in diameter, were so thickly coated with the scale that at a little distance they appeared as if they had been whitewashed." I have frequently seen apple and pear trees in nurseries in Massachusetts so badly infested as to have the appearance described by Dr. Lintner. This species is also occasionally injurious to currant and Japanese quince, and Dr. L. O. Howard reports it as being so abundant on Mountain ash in the Catskill mountains that hardly a twig or branch was found uninfested. Prof. Webster has quoted Mr. R. B. Fulton, Oxford, Miss., as follows : " This insect has been ruinous to the black-cap raspberry in this vicinity for the last three or four years. Old raspberry plants have been dug up and thrown away to get rid of the pest. . . . It multiplies so fast that it seems useless to try to kill it by any application to the plant."

Various authors have already published this species as infesting apple, pear, cherry, currant, Japan quince, crab-apple, black cherry, choke cherry, mountain ash, European mountain ash, peach and. black walnut. Mr. King of Lawrence, Mass., has sent me specimens on *Rhamnus catharticus* and *Clethra alnifolia*. Mr. Kirkland has informed me of its occurrence on *Pyrus arbutifolia, P. nigra, P. heterophylla, P. salicifolia pendula, P. floribunda, P. spectabilis* and *P. pinnatifolia*. Prof. Osborn recorded it on black-cap raspberry and Morgan on *Ribes sanguineum*.

The female usually lays from thirty to fifty eggs though Dr. Howard has recorded seventy-five. The eggs are laid in the fall and hatch in the latter part of May or early in June in the northern part of the United States, while in the latitude of Washington, D. C., Dr. Howard has found them hatching "quite uniformly" about the middle of May. There is only one generation in the northern part of the country, though it is probable that farther south, two or perhaps three occur. Walsh found that in Illinois the eggs are not laid "until about the end of September or sometimes in October."

Usually the species confines its attacks to the twigs of the tree though occasionally it spreads to the leaves also. Specimen twigs of Japanese quince from the Department of Agriculture bear both male and female scales on the leaves. Mr. Kirkland also called my attention to the same peculiarity.

There seems to be a very general tendency among the *Diaspinae* to secrete the scale underneath the epidermis of the bark or leaves of the host-plant whenever it is possible. While this overlying epidermis is usually readily seen with the naked eye, it is sometimes so obscure that it can be seen only by means of a hand lens or compound microscope. It sometimes happens that this overlying foreign matter gives a species a very different appearance when on different food plants, and this difference in appearance has led some authors to establish new varieties. *Howardia biclavis detecta* was founded on the absence of the overlying epidermis on the female scale while it is present in typical *biclavis*. Mr. Geo. B. King who has kindly sent me some very desirable scale insects, quite recently established the variety *Chionaspis furfurus fulvus* taken on *Rhamnus catharticus*, because of the unusual color of the overlying epidermis. It does not seem advisable in any case to give new names to scale insects because of a difference of appearance due entirely to foreign matter.

A parasite, *Alberus clisiocampae* (Ashmead), has been bred by Dr. Howard from this insect. Saunders observed a mite, *Tyroglyphus malus* and Gillette a Coccinellid beetle, *Hyperaspidius* sp. also feeding on the species. Various authors have recorded *Chilocorus bivulnerus* as predaceous upon it. The natural enemies of *C. furfura*, particularly *C. bivulnerus* hold this insect in check so that remedial measures are rarely necessary.

CHIONASPIS PINIFOLIAE.

Aspidiotus pinifoliae Fitch, Tr. N. Y. St. Ag'l. Soc., Vol. XV., p. 488 (1856).

Aspidiotus pinifoliae Fitch, Sec. Rep. Nox. Benif. Ins. N. Y. (1856).

Aspidiotus pinifoliae Fitch, Tr. N. Y. St. Ag'l. Soc., Vol. XVII., p. 741 (1858).

Aspidiotus pinifoliae Fitch, Fourth Rep. Nox. Benif. Ins. N. Y. (1858).

Aspidiotus pinifoliae Walsh. Pract. Ent., Vol. I., p. 90 (1866).

Mytilaspis pinifoliae LeBaron, First Ann. Rep. Nox. Ins. Ill., p. 83 (1871).

Mytilaspis pinifolii LeBaron, Sec. Ann. Rep. Nox. Ins. Ill., p. 161 (1872).

Mytilaspis pinifoliae Riley, Fifth Ann. Rep. Nox. Benif. Ins. Mo., p. 97 (1873).

Mytilaspis pinifoliae Bessey, Rep. Ia. State Ag'l. Soc., 1874, p. 232 (1875.)

Chionaspis pinifoliae Comstock, Ann. Rep. U. S. Dept. Agr., 1880, p. 318 (1881).

Mytilaspis pinifoliae Packard, Ins. Inj. to Forest and Shade Trees, Bull. 7, U. S. Ent. Com., p. 218 (1881).

Chionaspis pinifolii Riley, Am. Nat., Vol. XVI., p. 514 (1882).

Chionaspis pinifoliae Saunders, Rep. Ent. Soc. Ont., 1883, p. 52 (1884).

Chionaspis pinifoliae Lintner, Sec. Ann. Rep. Inj. Ins. N. Y., p. 184 (1885).

Chionaspis pinifolii Lintner, Fifth Ann. Rep. Inj. Ins. N. Y., p. 266 (1889).

Mytilaspis pinifoliae Packard, Fifth Rep. U. S. Ent. Com., p. 805 (1890).

Chionaspis pinifoliae Lintner, Seventh Ann. Rep. Inj. Ins. N. Y., p. 384 (1891).

Chionaspis pinifoliae Lintner, Ninth Ann. Rep. Inj. Ins. N. Y., p. 376 (1893).

Chionaspis pinifoliae Howard, Bull. U. S. Dept. Agr., Div. Ent., Tech. Ser. No. 1, pp. 13, 22, 52 (1895).

Chionaspis pinifoliae Comstock, Man. Study Ins., p. 174 (1895).

Chionaspis pinifolii Gillette and Baker, List Hemipt. Colo., Bull. Colo. Ag'l. Expt. Sta., No. 31, p. 129 (1895).

Chionaspis pinifoliae Lintner, Tenth Ann. Rep. Inj. Ins. N. Y., p. 518 (1895).

Chionaspis pinifolii Lintner, Eleventh Ann. Rep. Inj. Ins. N. Y., p. 203 (1896).

Chionaspis pinifolii Cockerell, Bull. N. Mex. Ag'l. Expt. Sta., No. 24, p. 38 (1896).

Chionaspis pinifoliae Osborn, Proc. Ia. Acad. Sci., Vol. V., p. 224 (1898).

Chionaspis pinifoliae Gillette, Bull. Colo. Ag'l. Expt. Sta., No. 47, p. 36 (1898).

Chionaspis pinifolii Pettit, Bull. Mich. Ag'l. Expt. Sta., No. 160, p. 415 (1898).

EGG.—Length, .25 mm. Ellipsoidal in form ; purplish in color.

LARVA.—Length, .3 mm. Oval in outline, broadest anteriorly and red in color.

SCALE OF FEMALE.—Plate 2, Figs. 4 and 4 B. Length, 3—4 mm. Usually nearly parallel-sided, as in *Mytilaspis*, but occasionally broadened posteriorly, as in other species of Chionaspis. Strongly convex ; moderately thick in texture ; snow-white in color often with a glossy surface. Exuviae 1 mm. long. First exuvia nearly colorless ; second, generally bright orange but occasionally dull yellowish-brown.

FEMALE.—Plate 7, Fig. 8. *Lobes* thin, almost transparent, striate, entire ; all well developed. Median lobes separated by a distance equal to about one-third the width of a lobe. Second and third pairs with the inner lobule larger. The *gland-spines* are arranged as follows : 1, 1, 1, 1, 1-2, 1-3. Moderately long, those nearest the median lobes and those in the fifth group being shortest. Both *spines* near the median lobes short and small, and other dorsal ones quite long. Second row of *dorsal gland-orifices* represented only by the anterior group consisting of 2—4 orifices. Third row with 4—5 orifices in the anterior and 4—6 in the posterior group. Fourth row with 3—7 orifices in the anterior and 6—10 in the posterior group. Median group of *circumgenital gland-orifices*, 7—13 ; anterior laterals, 12—21 ; posterior laterals, 14—19.

SCALE OF MALE.—Plate 2, Fig. 4 A.   Length, 1—1.1 mm.   Slightly broadened posteriorly, smooth in texture, tri-carinate.   Exuvia pale yellow or colorless, occupying about one-third the length of the scale.

MALE*.—Length of body including style .3 mm.; length of style .2 mm.   Uniformly pale red.   Eyes black.   Antennae as long as the body, ten-jointed; first two joints short and thick, the others longer, subequal except for the tenth which is shorter.   Wings large, longer than the body.   Antennae and legs bristly.

REMARKS.

This species is a native of this country.   It has been recorded from Maine, New York, New Jersey, District of Columbia, Michigan, Iowa, Illinois, Missouri, New Mexico, Florida, Colorado and California.   There are also specimens in the Department of Agriculture from Ohio and Washington Territory.   It is a very common species in Massachusetts and has also been sent me from Toronto, Ont., Canada.   Though the species usually exists in comparatively harmless numbers, it occasionally becomes abundant enough to be very destructive.   The fact that it produces two broods tends naturally to make it injurious.   Trees on which it has become very abundant have a distinct whitish appearance at a distance, as if sprinkled with snow.   Such trees are sometimes said to be affected by " white malady."   I have in many cases received leaves of pine and spruce almost completely covered by this species and Dr. Lintner has seen hundreds on a single leaf of *Pinus austriaca* in Washington Park, Albany, N. Y.   He states that a number of these trees were nearly killed by this scale insect.

The insect confines itself to coniferous trees and has been recorded by various authors on *Pinus strobus*, *P. resinosa*, *P. excelsa*, *P. mitis*, *P. cembra*, *P. pyrenaica*, *P. laricis*, *P. sylvestris*, *P. austriaca* and *P. pumilio*.   The Department of Agriculture contains examples on *Pseudotsuga taxifolia* and *Abies excelsa* and I have received specimens on *Abies nigra* from Canada and *Abies alba* from Massachusetts.

In the northern part of the United States the insect is two-brooded and passes the winter in the egg stage, twenty to seventy eggs being

---

*In the preparation of the description of this sex I have had for examination numerous dead and shrivelled specimens stuck to paper points.   The color is that given by Walsh.

sheltered under each scale. The first brood of young hatches about the middle of May. I have seen the eggs hatching at Amherst, Mass., on May 25, while LeBaron has seen them hatching from May 10 to May 25, and Dr. Riley as early as April 25. According to LeBaron the first eggs which hatch produce only male insects, while those which hatch last produce only females. The larvae crawl about over the leaves for two or three days and then come to rest and begin feeding. According to the observations of the author above quoted the male larvae settle entirely on the old leaves while the females usually migrate to the tender leaves at the ends of twigs. It would seem that this is not a fixed habit, however, as I have repeatedly watched this insect and have never found this marked difference in the place of settling of the two sexes. Le-Baron attributed the habit, as he observed it, to instinct on the part of the female larvae prompting them to take up their abode on the young leaves which would not drop to the ground before the insects had time to develop and produce young. The male insect requires ten days for the development of its scale while the female requires three weeks. Moreover, as has been said, the males hatch first and are therefore first to begin the formation of their scales. The male develops so much more rapidly than the female that it is mature just at the time the female is accomplishing its second molt, immediately after which copulation takes place.

It is almost impossible to separate the two broods of this insect, the time of hatching extending over so long a period, for scales in all stages of development can be found at any time during the summer. In fact I am not at all sure that there is not a partial or complete third brood even in this latitude. LeBaron discovered that by July the females had completed their development and had commenced laying eggs. These eggs began hatching by the first of August and continued till the middle of September. These eggs produce the second brood of larvae and the adult females resulting from them produce the eggs which, after remaining in that stage through the winter, hatch into the first brood of the following season. Necessarily, from the protracted season of egg-laying during the summer the development of the second brood is very irregular and no precise dates can be given. I have, however, seen living

3

females at Amherst, Mass., which were just completing the process of laying eggs on December 6.

Dr. Howard has reared *Perissopterus pulchellus* and both Dr. Riley and Dr. Howard have reared *Aphelines mytilaspidis* from this scale insect. *Chilocorus bivulnerus* has been repeatedly recorded as feeding on it and Dr. Riley has observed the Nitidulid beetle, *Cybocephalus nigritulus*, *Scymnus* sp., *Coccinella picta* and *Chrysopa* sp. in the same act.

CHIONASPIS PINIFOLIAE HETEROPHYLLAE.

Chionaspis pinifoliae heterophyllae Cooley, Can. Ent., Vol. XXIX., p. 281 (1897).

Chionaspis pinifoliae heterophyllae Berlese, Riv. di Pat. Veg., Vol. VI., p. 379 (1898).

This variety is indistinguishable from typical *C. pinifoliae* except by the lobes of the pygidium, a description of which is given below.

FEMALE.—Plate 7, Fig. 4. Median *lobes* rather small, sometimes scarcely perceptible, rounded at the extremities ; divergent, forming a distinct notch in the edge of the pygidium on the median line. Second and third pairs decidedly reduced; third pair sometimes wholly wanting; the two lobules of each lobe distinctly separated at their bases. See Pl. 7, Fig. 4. The lobes of this variety differ from those of *C. pinifoliae* in being much smaller and less distinct. In *pinifoliae* the median lobes are large and almost spatulate in form while in *C. pinifoliae heterophyllae* they are small and narrow. While the median lobes of this insect form a distinct notch, this is quite different from the notch in the genus *Phenacaspis*.

REMARKS.

This variety was originally described from specimens on Cuban pine, *Pinus heterophylla*, sent me by Prof. Quaintance from Florida. The Department of Agriculture contains examples on *Pinus sylvestris* from Providence, R. I., and on *Pinus mitis* from St. George, Fla. On Cuban pine the insects usually occur at the base of the very long slender leaves. I have also seen specimens on the bark of the young succulent twigs.

CHIONASPIS STANOTOPHRI n. sp.

SCALE OF FEMALE.—Plate 3, Fig. 7. Length, 2.2—2.6 mm. Moderately elongated, distinctly convex, firm in texture, clear white in color. Exuviae .8 mm. long; lemon-yellow or orange-yellow in color.

FEMALE.—Plate 8, Fig. 9. Three pairs of *lobes* are present. Median pair rounded, divergent, striate, entire; separated at their bases by a distance nearly equal to the width of one of the lobes. Lobules of the second pair rounded, entire, striate. Third pair varying in degree of development; composed of two broad, short, striate, entire lobules. The lobes are very slightly, if at all, darker than the remainder of the pygidium. In general appearance the median lobes resemble those of *pinifoliae* but they are further apart. The *gland-spines* are arranged as follows: 1-2, 1-2, 1-2, 3. There are four distinct spines at the base of each of the median lobes, two above and two below. Second row of *dorsal gland-orifices* represented by the anterior group consisting of 1—4 orifices. Third row with 4 orifices in the anterior and 5—6 in the posterior group. Fourth row with 4 orifices in the anterior and 5—6 in the posterior group. Median group of *circumgenital gland-orifices*, 7—12; anterior laterals, 18—24; posterior laterals, 15—17.

SCALE OF MALE.—Plate 3, Fig. 7 A. Length, 1—1.2 mm.; distinctly tri-carinate. Exuvia lemon-yellow or brownish, occupying scarcely one-third the length of the scale.

REMARKS.

On Buffalo grass, *Stanotophrum glabrum*, at Cape Town, South Africa. Collected and sent to me by Mr. C. P. Lounsbury to whom I am deeply indebted not only for this, but also for many other species of scale insects.

The appearance of the scales on the inside of the blades of grass where they are exclusively found might lead one to mistake this species for *Chionaspis spartinae* Comst. There is no perceptible ventral scale, however, in this species, while there is a very distinct one in *spartinae*. There are also important differences in the pygidia of the two insects.

CHIONASPIS PLATANI n. sp.

SCALE OF FEMALE.—Plate 3, Fig. 2. Length, 1.8—2 mm. Moderately broadened posteriorly, dirty white in color. Exuviae .7—.9 mm. long, pale yellowish-brown.

FEMALE.—Plate 7, Fig. 5. Median *lobes* large, well developed, divergent, with conspicuously serrate edges. Second pair well developed and with the outer lobule much smaller than the inner and often obscurely pointed ; obscurely serrate or entire. Third pair with the inner lobule usually well developed but sometimes rudimentary ; outer lobule very obscure or absent. The outer lobules are often of such a shape as to produce what appears to be a median notch. Examination of a series of specimens, however, shows the species to be a true member of this genus and not of *Phenacaspis* where it would be placed if it possessed a true median notch. The *gland-spines* are arranged as follows : 1, 1, 1, 1, 2-4. The one next the median, on each side, is very small, often almost invisible. Those on the anterior part of the pygidium are about equal to the median lobes in length. The *spines* are large and conspicuous. Second row of *dorsal gland-orifices* represented only by the anterior group consisting of 2—3 orifices. Third row with 4—6 orifices in the anterior and 2—4 in the posterior group. Fourth row with 4—8 orifices in the anterior and 4—6 in the posterior group. Median group of *circumgenital gland-orifices*, 6—13 ; anterior laterals, 10—17; posterior laterals, 10--16.

SCALE OF MALE.—Plate 3, Fig. 2 A. Length, .8—.9 mm. Parallel-sided to oval in outline. Occasionally very feebly unicarinate but usually without carinae. Exuvia pale yellowish-brown, occupying about two-fifths of the length of the scale.

REMARKS.

This species can be readily distinguished from all others in the genus by the large, divergent and plainly serrate median lobes. The only locality in which the species is known to occur is Riley Co., Kansas where Mr. P. J. Parrott collected it on sycamore. I am indebted to him for the specimens from which the foregoing descriptions were made.

CHIONASPIS HERBAE.

Chionaspis herbae Green, Coccidae of Ceylon, Part II., p. 132 (1899).
EGG.—" Eggs numerous, bright yellow." (Green).
SCALE OF FEMALE.—Plate 3, Fig. 5. Length, 2—2.75 mm.
Moderately broadened, white, opaque. Exuviae .9 mm. long, yellowish, brownish or almost colorless.

FEMALE.—Plate 7, Fig. 2. *Lobes* scarcely darker than the rest of the pygidium; striate, more or less serrate, the third pair usually more distinctly so than the others. Median pair rounded or obscurely pointed. Lobules of the third pair broad and short. The *gland-spines* are arranged as follows : 1, 1, 1, 1, 3-4. Second row of *dorsal gland-orifices* with the anterior group only present, numbering 2—3 ; third row with 2—3 orifices in the anterior and 7—9 in the posterior group. Median group of *circumgenital gland-orifices*, 11—16 ; anterior laterals, 20—27 ; posterior laterals, 14—26.

SCALE OF MALE.—Plate 3, Fig. 5 A. Length, 1.1—1.3 mm.
Distinctly tri-carinate with the surface rough. Exuvia pale yellow.

MALE.—" Adult male bright red. Ocelli black. Rudimentary eyes on genae obscurely but unmistakably compound, surrounded by a ring of pigment spots. Antennae with a single knobbed hair at apex. Foot with three digitules, one ungual and two tarsal. Length, .60 mm." (Green).

REMARKS.

Found on stems and leaves of *Panicum* sp., *Ischaemum ciliare*, *Ophismenus compositus* and various other grasses in Ceylon. My specimens were sent me by Mr. Green, the author of the species.

CHIONASPIS DYSOXYLI.

Chionaspis dysoxyli Maskell, Trans. N. Z.Inst.,Vol. XVII.,p. 22(1884).
Chionaspis dysoxyli Maskell, Ins. Nox. to Agr. and Plants in N. Z.,
p. 55 (1887).
Chionaspis dysoxyli Maskell, Trans. N. Z. Inst., Vol. XXII., p. 135
• (1889).
Chionaspis dysoxyli Maskell, Trans. N. Z. Inst., Vol. XXVII., p. 50
(1894).

SCALE OF FEMALE.—Plate 3, Fig. 6. Length, 2—2.5 mm. Distinctly broadened posteriorly, moderately thick, pure white, or, when occurring on the stem and covered with epidermis, dirty white. Exuviae .9 mm. long, pale orange-yellow, often with an indefinite black spot in the middle of the second exuvia. First exuvia overlying the second more than half its length. The second exuvia is very thin and the dark spot in the middle, when present, is due to the dead body of the female showing through. In describing the scale Maskell says, "with a faint pink tinge when the egg-mass beneath shows through."

FEMALE.—Plate 8, Fig. 1. Median *lobes* moderately well developed, set closely together, rounded, entire. Second and third pairs with the inner lobule longer and rounded and the outer lobule smaller and bluntly pointed; entire. The *gland-spines* are arranged as follows: 1, 1, 1, 1, 3-4. The first gland-spine is nearly as long as the others. Second row of *dorsal gland-orifices* usually absent but occasionally represented by the posterior group consisting of about two orifices. Third row with 1—3 orifices in the anterior and 3—5 in the posterior group. Fourth row with 1—2 orifices in the anterior and 5 in the posterior group. Median group of *circumgenital gland orifices*, 7—9; anterior laterals, 11—16; posterior laterals, 7—2

SCALE OF MALE.—Plate 3, Fig. 6 A. Length, .8—1 mm. Parallel-sided, very distinctly tri-carinate. Exuvia orange-yellow, extending about one-third of the length of the scale.

REMARKS.

This species can be distinguished from others in the genus by the small yet distinct lobes and the thinness of the second exuvia. The exuviae resemble those of *Phenacaspis cockerelli* Cooley. *C. dysoxyli* has been taken only in New Zealand where it appears to be abundant and injurious. Maskell says of it: "The large white puparia of this insect do much to spoil the appearance of *Dysoxylon*, one of the most showy-leaved plants in New Zealand." The species is most frequently found on the leaves and often occurs clustered along the midrib. The food plants are *Dysoxylon spectabile, Hoheria angustifolia* and *Melicytus tamifrons*.

CHIONASPIS WISTARIAE.

Chionaspis wistariae Cooley, Can. Ent., Vol. XXIX., p. 280 (1897).
Chionaspis wistariae Berlese, Rivista di Patologia Vegetale, Vol. VI.,
p. 379 (1898).

SCALE OF FEMALE.—Plate 2, Fig. 5. Length, 1.8—2.3 mm.
Plainly broadened posteriorly, rather thin in texture, dirty white in
color. Exuviae .8 mm. long, brown.

FEMALE.—Plate 7, Fig. 7. Median *lobes* larger and more conspicuous in proportion to the other lobes than is usual in this genus;
usually parallel in general direction, though sometimes slightly divergent; rounded or indistinctly pointed at the extremities, firmly united
at their bases, the chitinous thickened process which unites them
extending anteriorly for a distance about equal to the length of the
lobes. Second pair distinct and entire but much smaller than the
median pair; outer lobule smaller than the inner. Third pair usually
obsolete but sometimes represented by low, serrate prominences.
The *gland-spines* are arranged as follows: 1, 1, 1, 1, 1-2, 2-4. The
first one is short and blunt, scarcely surpassing the median lobes.
Second row of *dorsal gland-orifices* represented only by the anterior
group consisting of 2—3 orifices. Third row with 3—4 orifices in
the anterior and 4—5 in the posterior group. Fourth row with 3—4
orifices in the anterior and 4—6 in the posterior group. Median
group of *circumgenital gland-orifices*, 8—15; anterior laterals, 19—31;
posterior laterals, 13—23.

SCALE OF MALE.—Plate 2, Fig. 5 A. Length, about 1 mm. Sides
nearly parallel, distinctly tri-carinate. Exuvia yellowish-brown,
occupying about one-third of the length of the scale.

REMARKS.

This insect is readily distinguished from all others of the genus
by the median lobes. The only insect which approaches it is *C.
platani* but in that species the median lobes are longer and more
plainly serrate. In *C. wistariae* the male scale is very plainly carinated. while in *C. platani* it is very feebly carinated or without
carinae.

So far as I know the species has never been collected since Mr. Alexander Craw took it on the bark of *Wistaria* arriving at San Francisco from Japan in July 1897. These were the specimens from which the species was originally described.

CHIONASPIS CARYAE.

Chionaspis caryae Cooley, Can. Ent., Vol. XXX., p. 86 (1898).

Chionaspis caryae Berlese, Riv. di Pat. Veg., Vol. VI., p. 379 (1898).

SCALE OF FEMALE.—Plate 2, Fig. 3. Length, 1.7—2. mm. Irregular in form, thick in texture, dirty white in color; inconspicuous on the bark of the host-plant. Exuviae .7 mm. long, dark brown. The first exuvia readily distinguishable, the second almost hidden from view by the copious secretion which covers it.

FEMALE.—Plate 8, Fig. 5. Median *lobes* large, distinct, entire; with the inner edges fused to near the ends of the lobes. Often with a club-shaped chitinous process extending anteriorly from them on the median line. Second and third pairs more or less serrate; inner lobule larger than the outer. Outer lobule of the third lobe often nearly obsolete. The *gland-spines* are arranged as follows: 1, 1, 1, 1-2, 5-7. The first one is short and blunt. Second row of *dorsal gland-orifices* represented only by the anterior group consisting of 1—4 orifices. Third row with 4—5 orifices in the anterior and 3—5 in the posterior group. Fourth row with 4—6 orifices in the anterior and 4—5 in the posterior group. Median group of *circumgenital gland-orifices*, 12—19, anterior laterals, 21—29; posterior laterals, 15—22.

SCALE OF MALE.—Plate 2, Fig. 3 A. Length, .5—.7 mm. Elliptical in outline with a very distinct median carina. Exuvia pale brown, occupying about one-third of the length of the scale.

REMARKS.

This species has no near relatives so far as is known, the only insect resembling it being *C. americana*, which also has the inner edges of the median lobes fused together. The two species can be readily distinguished by the lobes, in *C. americana* being distinctly notched, while in *C. caryae* they are entire. There are also other important differences.

The specimens from which the foregoing descriptions were made are in the Department of Agriculture and were collected on the bark of " Hickory " at Washington, D. C.

CHIONASPIS AMERICANA.

Chionaspis americana (Johnson MS.) Howard, Bull. U.S. Dept. Agr., Div. Ent., Tech. Ser. No. 1, p. 44 (1895).

Chionaspis americana Johnson, Ent. News, Vol. VII., p. 150 (1896).

Chionaspis americana Johnson, Bull. Ill. St. Lab. Nat. Hist., Vol. IV., p. 390 (1896).

Chionaspis americana Lugger, First Ann. Rep. Ent. Minn., p. 129 (1896).

EGG.—Slightly more than .2 mm. long; ellipsoidal; purplish.

LARVA*.—Length .22 mm.; width .13 mm.; Ovate in outline, broadest posteriorly. Red. Anal filaments distinct except at the base; about as long as the width of the body. A row of dark spots along the lateral margin posteriorly.

SCALE OF FEMALE.—Plate 2, Fig. 6. Length, 2—3.2 mm. Usually broadest near the middle. Plainly convex, moderately thick in texture. The color of the scale itself is pure white but it is often coated by a black sooty substance or by the epidermis of the bark which affects the general color and often obscures the scale from view. Exuviae .7 mm. long, brown, often almost completely hidden from view by the superficial coatings above mentioned. When removed from the bark a conspicuous white scar is left.

FEMALE.—Plate 8, Figs. 3 and 4. Broadest toward the posterior end; yellow or brownish, the central portion darkened and of a purplish tinge when containing eggs. Median and second pairs of *lobes* well developed and distinct; third pair sometimes well developed and sometimes very obscure or absent. A club-shaped process extending anteriorly from between the median lobes. Median lobes

---

*The description of the larva is made from Johnson's description and my own observation.

prominent, fused on their inner edges; with a distinct notch on the outer edge of each lobe. Second lobe obscurely divided into an inner and outer lobule. Inner lobule a little oblique, with one or two notches on the outer edges; outer lobule small, entire or with one notch. Third lobe, when present, faintly divided into two lobules; inner lobule with one faint notch or entire. The *gland-spines* are arranged as follows: 1, 1-2, 2, 2-4, 5-7. Those in the second and third groups are often forked at the tip. The first one is short, blunt or sometimes wanting. Second row of *dorsal gland-orifices* entirely absent. Third row with 4—6 orifices in the anterior and 4—5 in the posterior group. Median group of *circumgenital gland-orifices*, 20—30; anterior laterals, 18—42; posterior laterals, 20—30.

SCALE OF MALE.—Plate 2, Fig. 6 A. Length, .7—1 mm. Sides parallel; tri-carinate. Exuvia pale yellow, occupying about two-fifths of the length of the scale.

MALE.—Two forms of males occur in this species; one with fully developed and one with rudimentary wings. Both forms agree as follows: Length of body .25 to .35 mm. Reddish brown; eyes prominent; antennae yellowish or sometimes pinkish, ten-jointed, covered with stout transparent hairs. Legs stout, lighter in color than the body; tarsi sparsely hairy. Style about .2 mm. long, of about the same color as the legs.

In the form with fully developed wings, these organs extend, when folded over the back, a little beyond the tip of the style and the halteres are well developed. In the other form the wings are represented by mere stubs and the halteres are short and stout and lack the terminal hook. I have never seen the male insect and have arranged the foregoing description from that published by Johnson.

REMARKS.

The nearest relative of *C. americana* is *C. caryae*. The two species may be distinguished by the fact that in *C. americana* the median lobes are notched, while in *C. caryae* they are entire. This species is a native of North America and so far as known has been taken in no other country. Professor Johnson described it from specimens from Illinois and stated that it is found throughout that state and in Minnesota. The Department of Agriculture contains examples from Stillwater, Okla.; Belton, Tex.; Oswego and Edgerton, Kan.; Kansas City, Kirkwood and St. Louis, Mo.; Bristol, Conn., and Brooklyn, N. Y. It occurs throughout the state of Massachusetts.

This species sometimes becomes very abundant and destructive to some extent. Professor Johnson found it abundant on "virgin timber." It confines its attacks to elms and is most often found on *Ulmus americana* though I have taken it on *Ulmus montana* var. *camperdown pendula*. The insect passes the winter in the egg stage. At Amherst, Mass., the eggs hatch about the middle of May, the young all making their appearance within a short time of each other. Professor Johnson's observations show that the insect is two-brooded. The females confine themselves to the bark of the tree and can be found from the trunk to the very tips of the twigs. The males occur both on the bark and on the under side of the leaves. The female usually lays about seventy eggs but the number varies from a very few to about eighty-five.

Prof. Johnson bred two parasites, *Perissopterus pulchellus* and *Physcus varicornis,* from the species. He has also seen the larva and adult of *Chilocorus bivulnerus* feeding on it.

Genus HEMICHIONASPIS.

Hemichionaspis Cockerell, Am. Nat., Vol. XXXI., p. 592 (1897).

Hemichionaspis Cockerell, First Suppl. Check-list Coccidae ; Bull. Ill. St. Lab. Nat. Hist., Vol. V., p. 397 (1889).

SCALE OF FEMALE.—Plate 1, Fig. 4. More or less pyriform in outline, though sometimes elongated and narrow. Ventral scale only slightly developed. Exuviae at the anterior extremity, the first one partly overlying the second. First exuvia naked, second more or less covered by secreted matter. Secreted portion varying from white to brown or yellowish.

FEMALE. —Plate 6, Fig. 1. Elongated, broadened posteriorly, conspicuously segmented. Abdominal segments with a more or less distinct group of small nearly circular gland-orifices on each side, more distinct near the pygidium (Plate 6, Fig. 6.). More or less distinct rows of oval gland-orifices on the dorsal surface, between the segments. A group of gland-spines on each side of the abdominal segments, more distinct near the pygidium than anteriorly. The characters of the pygidium are as follows : One, two or three pairs of *lobes* present. Median lobes with their inner edges straight, parallel, and close to each other or touching for their entire length, the outer edges being rounded and either crenate or serrate. These two lobes together form approximately a semi-circle, and are darker than the other lobes (Plate 9, Fig. 9.). Lobes of the second and third pairs, when present, composed of two lobules of which the inner is larger than the outer. *Gland-spines* simple and usually quite large and conspicuous. *Spines* usually plainly visible ; those on the dorsal longer than those on the ventral surface. *Circumgenital gland-orifices* always present and arranged in five groups.

SCALE OF MALE.—Plate 1, Fig. 4 A. Elongated, uni-carinate or tri-carinate. Ventral scale complete forming with the upper part, a tube. Plate 1, Fig. 4 A represents the male scale of *aspidistrae*, the type of this genus. Plate 6, Fig. 7, shows it in cross section.

REMARKS.

This genus is, as a rule, tropical in its range of distribution though *aspidistrae* has been found far north of the tropics in greenhouses.

Prof. Cockerell in his original descriptive note adopted *aspidistrae* as the type of the genus.

SYNOPTIC TABLE OF SPECIES.

1. { Scale of female white, ... 2.
   { Scale of female brown or yellowish, . . . 4.

2. { Median lobes quite small; long and narrow. See Plate 9,
   { Fig. 1, ... *dracaenae.*
   { Median lobes large and broad, the two together being nearly
   { semi-circular in outline, ... 3.

3. { Marginal gland prominences quite well developed and drawn
   { out into a slender spine. See Plate 9, Figs. 2 and 4,
   { *scrobicularum.*
   { Marginal gland prominences not well developed, at least not
   { drawn out into spines. See Plate 9, Fig. 7, *rhododendri.*

4. { Median lobes crenate. See Plate 9, Fig. 5, . *minor.*
   { Median lobes serrate. See Plate 9, Fig. 6, *minor strachani.*

5. { Median lobes very large, dark colored and conspicuous. See
   { Plate 9, Fig. 10, ... *mussaendae.*
   { Median lobes small, somewhat sunken into the pygidium.
   { See Plate 9, Fig. 3, ... 6.

6. { Female scale unusually elongated (Plate 1, Fig. 3); second
   { exuvia long and narrow (Plate 1, Fig. 3). . . *theae.*
   { Female scale only moderately elongated (Plate 1, Fig. 4),
   { second exuvia not unusually long compared with its width
   { (Plate 1, Fig. 4), ... *aspidistrae.*

HEMICHIONASPIS ASPIDISTRAE.

Chionaspis aspidistrae Signoret, Ann. Soc. Ent. Fr.,Ser. 4, Vol. IX., p. 443 (1869).

Chionaspis brasiliensis Signoret, Ann. Soc. Ent. Fr., Ser. 4, Vol. IX., p. 444 (1869).

Chionaspis aspidistrae Maskell, Trans. N. Z. Inst., Vol. XXIV., p. 15 (1891).

Chionaspis aspidistrae Cotes, Ind. Mus. Notes, Vol. II., No. 1, p. 17 (1891).

Chionaspis aspidistrae Maskell, Ent. Mo. Mag., Vol. XXVII., p. 70 (1892).

Chionaspis brasiliensis Maskell, Trans. N. Z. Inst., Vol. XXV., p. 210 (1892).

Chionaspis brasiliensis Maskell, Trans. N. Z. Inst., Vol. XXVI., p. 68 (1893).

Chionaspis brasiliensis Cockerell, Jour. Trinidad Field Nat. Club, Vol. I., p. 306 (1894).

Chionaspis brasiliensis Cotes, Ind. Mus. Notes, Vol. III., No. 5, p. 52 (1894).

Chionaspis aspidistrae Cockerell, Proc. U. S. Nat'l.Mus., Vol. XVII., p. 620 (1895).

Chionaspis aspidistrae Newstead, Ent. Mo. Mag., Vol. XXXII., p. 60 (1896).

Chionaspis aspidistrae Maskell, Ent. Mo. Mag., Vol. XXXII., p. 223 (1896).

Chionaspis aspidistrae Maskell, Trans. N. Z. Inst., Vol. XXIX., p. 305 (1896).

Chionaspis aspidistrae Craw, Fifth Bien. Rep. St. Bd. Hort. Calif., p. 35 (1896).

Chionaspis latus Cockerell, Psyche, Vol. VII.,(Supplement), p. 21 (1896).

Chionaspis latus Cockerell, Bull. U. S. Dept. Agr., Div. Ent., Tech. Ser. 4, p. 53 (1896).

Chionaspis brasiliensis Cockerell, Bull. Bot. Dept. Jam., Vol. III., (N. S.), p. 257 (1896).

Chionaspis aspidistrae Craw, Bull. U. S. Dept. Agr., Div. Ent., Tech. Ser. 4, p. 40 (1896).

Chionaspis brasiliensis Green, Ind. Mus. Notes, Vol. IV., p. 1 (1896).

Chionaspis brasiliensis Maskell, Ent. Mo. Mag., Vol. XXXIII., p. 242 (1897).

Chionaspis aspidistrae Green, Ent. Mo. Mag., Vol. XXXIII., p. 70 (1897).

Chionaspis brasiliensis Cockerell, Am. Nat., Vol. XXXI., p. 592 (1897).

Egg.—According to Mr. Green the eggs are reddish-fulvous.

Larva.—Mr. Green states that the newly hatched larvae are pale yellow.

SCALE OF FEMALE.—Plate 4, Fig. 1. Length, 1.8—2.6 mm. Distinctly broadened posteriorly and usually broadly rounded at the extremity, but occasionally bluntly pointed. Very thin and delicate in texture or moderately thick and strong. Pale yellowish-brown to brown. Exuviae .7—.9 mm. long, of the same color as the secreted portion of the scale but slightly brighter.

FEMALE.—Plate 6, Fig. 1. The first four segments anterior to the pygidium very pronounced, being often produced at each side into a conspicuous protuberance. First and second pairs of *lobes* (Plate 9, Figs. 8 and 9) well developed, third pair very rudimentary or wanting. Each median lobe with three distinct notches on the outer curved edge. Lobules of the second lobe long and narrow, spatulate in form; edges thickened at the base. The *gland-spines* are arranged as follows: 1, 1, 1, 1, 2-5. As a rule the fifth group contains 2-3 spines, but in one specimen I observed 5. The *marginal gland-orifice* between the first and second lobes is situated on a large, conspicuous prominence. Second row of *dorsal gland-orifices* wholly absent. Third and fourth rows with 2—5 orifices in their posterior groups. Anterior groups absent. Median group of *circumgenital gland-orifices*, 5—15; anterior laterals, 15—22; posterior laterals, 17—23.

SCALE OF MALE.—Plate 1, Fig. 4 A. Length, 1—1.3 mm. Exuvia bright yellow.

REMARKS.

This species agrees with *theae* Mask. in having the female scale brown, but may be separated from that species by a broader second exuvia. Plate 6, Fig. 2 represents the second exuvia of *aspidistrae* and Fig. 3, of the same plate, *theae*. Superficially the female scale of *mussaendae* resembles the two species. In *mussaendae*, however, the median lobes are much larger and darker in color. In his original description of *aspidistrae*, Signoret did not state where his specimens were procured, hence we may reasonably infer that they were from France. He plainly states, however, that his specimens of *brasiliensis* were from Bahia, Brazil, and as this species is now considered a synonym of *aspidistrae*, it would seem that *aspidistrae* was originally known from France and Bahia, Brazil. It has since been found in Trinidad (Urich and Hart), Ceylon (Green), South Australia (Maskell), Formosa (Maskell), India (Maskell), England (Newstead), Japan (Craw and Cockerell), and California (Cockerell). In Part II., of his " Coccidae of Ceylon," p. 111, Green states that this is one of the most widely distributed species of the genus (meaning the genus Chionaspis in its widest sense) found in Ceylon. He also states in the same paragraph that it is a common greenhouse pest in Europe. I have taken this insect on various species of ferns in the greenhouses of the Department of Agriculture at Washington, D. C. Though reported from only two places in the United States, Washington, D. C., and California, it is probable that the species occurs in greenhouses in many other localities in this country.

This species was originally described from specimens on *Aspidistra* and an unknown plant. Maskell recorded it on *Orchia*, *Areca catechu* and *Thea*. Green took it on *Acacia melanoxylon*, *Strobilanthus viscosus*, *Capparis moorrii*, *Amcmum*, *Ficus*, *Cyanotus*, *Crotou*, *Alocasia*, *Pothos*. *Gaultheria fragrans*, *Cocos plumosa*, *Helichonia metallica*, "Pepper" and "Mango." Cockerell found it on "Orange" and various authors have taken it on different species of cultivated ferns.

This species has never been regarded as particularly destructive except in India and Ceylon where Mr. E. Cotes and Mr. E. E. Green have found it to be of considerable economic importance. Mr. Cotes writing in Indian Museum Notes, Vol. II., No. 1, p. 17(1891), states that examples were received from Mr. Marshall Woodrow of Poona which had been taken from Suparee nut palm, *Areca catechu*, in Janjira State, on the coast, about eighty miles south of Bombay. It was estimated that the productiveness of the affected trees had been reduced to one-tenth the usual amount. The trees had been suffering from attacks by this insect for twenty-five years and had been especially injured during the last six or seven years. The insects were determined as *aspidistrae* by Mr. Maskell. Green says, " The colonies are often very extensive and this species must be considered a distinctly injurious one. I have frequently seen young Areca palms in which every frond was covered on both sides with the insects, the fronds appearing yellow instead of green, from the multitude of discolored spots, each one of which marks the position of one of the insects."

The only natural enemy of *aspidistrae* of which I have found any record is the Coccinellid beetle, *Chilocorus circumdatus*, which Mr.

Green found doing good service in reducing the numbers of this scale insect. He says of it, " I have frequently found the remains of a large colony of this bug in which every scale had been opened and the contents devoured by this beetle, which is equally voracious in both the larval and adult stages."

An extended and critical study of examples of *lata* Ckll. and *brasiliensis* Sign. convinces me that they are synonyms of *aspidistrae* Sign. The specimens of *lata* Ckll. which I have had for examination are cotypes, of which a part were sent me by Prof. Cockerell, and a part were from the collections of the Department of Agriculture. In his original description of this species Cockerell lays particular stress on the shape of the female scale which is very broad for its length, and this character seemed to him sufficient to separate the specimens from other known species. My examination of the specimens convinced me that they were immature and that the scales had been only partly formed. I was led to this conclusion by the fact that no eggs or egg shells were found under the scales or within the bodies of the females. No appreciable structural differences could be found on the insects themselves by which to separate them from *aspidistrae*. A female scale of *lata* Ckll. is shown on Plate 1, Fig. 2. Various authors have suggested that *brasiliensis** should be placed as a synonym of *aspidistrae*, there being no structural differences of sufficient value to separate them. Having at my disposal a very long series of both *aspidistrae* and *brasiliensis* and having before me all that has been written on the affinities of the species I endeavored to trace out the distinctions by which Signoret separated the two species at the outset. This resulted in a total failure and led me to unite the two species under the name of *aspidistrae*, which by priority of position should be retained in preference to *brasiliensis* as Signoret's description of *aspidistrae* precedes that of *brasiliensis* in the same paper.

HEMICHIONASPIS MUSSAENDAE.

Chionaspis aspidistrae Sign. var. *mussaendae* Green, Ind. Mus. Notes, Vol. IV., p. 1 (1896).

*According to Mr. Newstead no cotypes of *brasiliensis* are preserved at the Hof-Museum at Vienna.

4

Chionaspis aspidistrae var. *mussaendae* Maskell, Ent. Mo. Mag., Vol. XXXII., p. 224 (1896).

Chionaspis aspidistrae var. *mussaendae* Maskell, Trans. N. Z. Inst., Vol. XXIX., p. 306 (1896).

Chionaspis mussaendae Green, Coccidae of Ceylon, Part II., p. 117 (1899).

EARLY STAGES.—"Eggs and young larvae brownish red." (Green).

SCALE OF FEMALE.—Plate 1, Fig. 1. Length, 2.4—2.3 mm. Elongated, broadened posteriorly, the anterior portion often quite narrow; grayish white in color. Exuviae .8—.6 mm. long, brown in color.

FEMALE.—Segmentation very distinct toward the posterior end of the body. Median *lobes* (Plate 9, Fig. 10) very large and conspicuous; crenate on their outer edges, the crenations gradually decreasing in size from the inner edge of each lobe outward. Second and third pairs of lobes absent. *Gland-spines* arranged as follows: 1, 1, 1, 1-2, 5-6. The one nearest the median lobes small and obscure. The *marginal gland-orifice* next to the median lobes is on a broad and conspicuous protuberance. The *dorsal gland-orifices* are few in number. Second row absent; third and fourth rows represented only by their posterior groups numbering 2—3 and 2—6 respectively. Median group of *circumgenital gland-orifices*, 17—29; anterior laterals, 26—40; posterior laterals, 22—35.

SCALE OF MALE.—Plate 1, Fig. 1 A. Length, 1.3 mm. Very distinctly tricarinate. Exuvia pale brownish-yellow.

MALE.—"Adult male bright brick-red. Form normal. Antennae with a single knobbed hair at extremity. Foot, with one tarsal and one ungual digitule. Tarsus nearly as long as tibia. Length rather more than 1 mm." (Green).

REMARKS.

Found in Ceylon on *Mussaenda frondosa* and occasionally on *Loranthus* and *Debregnesia*. The male scales occur crowded together in groups, each individual being attached to the bark only at the anterior extremity, the rest of the scale being elevated and lying on the backs of the scales next behind it.

Mr. Green states that the female insect is frequently parasitized by the minute hymenopteron, *Aphelinus diaspidis* How.

HEMICHIONASPIS THEAE.

Chionaspis theae Maskell, Ind. Mus. Notes, Vol. II., No. 1, p. 60 (1891).

Chionaspis theae Cotes, Ind. Mus. Notes, Vol. II., No. 6, p. 168 (1893).

Chionaspis theae Cockerell, Proc. U. S. Nat. Mus., Vol. XVII., p. 620 (1895).

Chionaspis exercitata Green, Ind. Mus. Notes, Vol. IV., No. 1, p. 2 (1896).

Chionaspis aspidistrae var. *theae* Maskell, Trans. N. Z. Inst., Vol. XXIX., p. 305 (1896).

Chionaspis theae Cotes, Ind. Mus. Notes, Vol. III., No. 1, pp. 24, 25 (1896).

Chionaspis theae Cotes, Ind. Mus. Notes, Vol. III., No. 4, pp. 39, 60 (1896).

Chionaspis theae Green, Coccidae of Ceylon, Part II., p. 113 (1899).

EARLY STAGES.—"Eggs and larvae dull red." (Green).

SCALE OF FEMALE.—Plate 1, Fig. 3. Length, 2 mm. Usually quite narrow though occasionally as broad as in *aspidistrae*; brown. Exuviae .9 mm. long, of the same color as the secreted portion.

FEMALE.—Elongated, rather narrow; segmentation indistinct except toward the posterior end where it is extended into broad prominences. Plate 6, Fig. 4. Median and second pairs of *lobes* present. Plate 9, Fig. 3. Median pair rather small, as in *aspidistrae*, distinctly crenate, brown. Lobes of the second pair divided into two spatulate lobules, the inner one being longer than the outer. The *gland-spines* nearest the median lobes are small and obscure while those on the anterior part of the pygidium are large and conspicuous, those between being intermediate in size. They are arranged as follows: 1, 1, 1, 1-2, 2. The *marginal gland-orifice* between the median and second lobe on each side is situated on a conspicuous prominence. The *dorsal gland-orifices* are few in number. Second row wholly absent; third and fourth rows represented only by their posterior groups, numbering 1—2 orifices each, Median group of *circumgenital gland-orifices*, 6—7; anterior laterals. 13—15; posterior laterals, 10—13.

SCALE OF MALE.—Plate 1, Fig. 3 A. Length, 1—1.2 mm. Very distinctly tri-carinated. Exuvia brownish-yellow.

MALE.—"Adult male bright red; apodema paler; legs yellowish. Ocelli large, black; lower pair separated by nearly their own diameter. Rudimentary eyes not apparent. Antennae as long as the body of the insect. Tenth joint much shorter than the ninth, a curved knobbed hair at its apex. Foot with two digitules (one ungual and one tarsal). Tarsus as long as tibia. Length about 1 mm." (Green).

REMARKS.

This species can be readily distinguished from *aspidistrae*, its nearest relative, by the second exuvia being quite narrow and elongated. See Plate 6, Figs. 2 and 3.

This species was originally described from specimens on tea from Kangra Valley, Northern India. Mr. Green has also found it in Ceylon on *Pyscatoria* as well as on tea. This species has not been reported as causing very much damage, though its presence on the tea plants seems to have caused some apprehension among the growers.

The male scales occur in groups, the different individuals lying with their anterior extremities all pointing in the same direction, the scales being in parallel positions.

Mr. Cotes has recorded the small Hymenopterous parasite *Aphelinus theae* Cotes, as an enemy to this scale insect.

HEMICHIONASPIS MINOR.

Chionaspis minor Maskell, Trans. N. Z. Inst., Vol. XVII., p. 33 (1884).

Chionaspis minor Maskell, Ins. Nox. to Agr. and Plants in N. Z., p. 56 (1887).

Chionaspis minor Maskell, Trans. N. Z. Inst., Vol. XXV., p. 210 (1892).

Chionaspis minor Cockerell, Ent. Mo. Mag., Vol. XXIX., p. 17 (1893).

Chionaspis minor Cockerell, Ins. Life, Vol. V., pp. 160, 246 (1893).

Chionaspis timidus Riley & Howard, Ins. Life, Vol. VI., p. 50 (1893).

Chionaspis angustior Riley & Howard, Ins. Life, Vol. VI., p. 50 (1893).

Chionaspis minor Riley & Howard, Ins. Life, Vol., VI., p. 50 (1893).

Chionaspis minor Cockerell, Ins. Life, Vol. VI., pp. 102, 103 (1893).

Chionaspis minor Maskell, Trans. N. Z. Inst., Vol. XXVII., p. 10 (1894).

Chionaspis minor Cockerell, Ent. News, Vol. VI., p. 157 (1895).

Chionaspis minor Cockerell, Bull. Bot. Dept. Jam., Vol. III. (N. S.), p. 257 (1896).

Chionaspis minor Cockerell, Jour. Trinidad Field Nat. Club., Vol. II., p. 307 (1896).

Chionaspis minor Cooley, Can. Ent., Vol. XXX., p. 89 (1898).

Chionaspis albizziae Green, Coccidae of Ceylon, Part II., p. 115 (1899).

EGG.—"Orange, numerous." (Cockerell).

SCALE OF FEMALE.—Plate 3, Fig. 4. Length, 1.8—2.3 mm. Elongated, broadened posteriorly. Moderately thick in texture, white. Exuviae .7 mm. long, yellowish-brown.

FEMALE.—Plate 6, Fig. 8. Median *lobes* distinctly darker than the rest of the pygidium ; outer edge of each divided into from two to four crenations. Second pair rudimentary or wanting ; occasionally fairly well developed. Third pair wanting. The *gland-spines* are arranged as follows : 1, 1, 1, 1, 2-3. The *marginal gland-orifice* nearest the median lobes is situated on a broad conspicuous prominence. *Dorsal gland-orifices* few in number. Second row wholly absent. Third and fourth rows with posterior groups numbering 1—3, their anterior groups being either absent or replaced by small and obscure almost circular orifices. Median group of *circumgenital gland-orifices*, 6—11 ; anterior laterals, 12—20 ; posterior laterals, 10—18.

SCALE OF MALE.—Plate 3, Fig. 4 A. Length, .9 mm. Very distinctly tri-carinate. Exuvia yellowish-brown.

REMARKS.

This insect was first found in New Zealand from which country Maskell originally described it. Cockerell has frequently recorded it from the West Indies and I have also published its occurrence in Panama and Florida. The species is very common in the West Indies and it is probable that these islands are its original home.

Maskell has taken the insect on *Parsonia, Rhipogonum scandens*; Cockerell on Hibiscus, Capsicum, Pelargonium, "Cotton," "Pepper," "Cocoanut-palm" and I have recorded it on *Melia azedarach* also.

Of its destructiveness Cockerell says, "From its frequent abundance, it becomes quite troublesome on garden plants." I have been informed by Prof. Quaintance that the species severely attacks the "China-trees" (*Melia azedarach*) at Braidentown, Fla. and many trees were said to have been apparently killed by it. From what we know of the species it must be considered a very injurious one. From the above list of food plants it will be seen that the insect has been known to attack cotton plants and should it become established in the cotton fields of our southern states it might prove a serious pest.

Cockerell's unpublished variety *timida* I believe to be a synonym of *minor* for reasons given in the remarks under *Chionaspis furfura*. Green's species *albizziae* to the best of my knowledge should also be placed as a synonym of *minor*, as I am unable to separate the two. I have had for examination specimens of *albizziae* received direct from Mr. Green. I regret that I was unable to inform him of my conclusion regarding this insect before his manuscript on the species for Part II., of his "Coccidae of Ceylon" had gone to press. I think it probable that Mr. Green has never had specimens of *minor* for examination.

Mr. Green states that *albizziae* is extensively preyed upon by the Coccinellid beetle, *Chilocorus circumdatus* and is also parasitized by the hymenopterous insects, *Prospalta aurantii* and *Aphelinus diaspidis*.

HEMICHIONASPIS MINOR STRACHANI n. var.

This variety differs from typical *minor* in having the exuviae of the female scale rather darker and contrasting more strongly with the secreted portion, and in having the median lobes broader in proportion to their length and more finely and less distinctly crenate. See Plate 9, Fig. 6.

REMARKS.

On an unknown plant from Aboekuta, Egbaland, West Africa. Collected by Dr. Henry Strachan and sent to Prof. Cockerell who turned the specimens over to me.

HEMICHIONASPIS SCROBICULARUM.

Chionaspis scrobicularum Green, Coccidae of Ceylon, Part II., p. 121 (1899).

EARLY STAGES.—"Eggs and larvae pale yellow." (Green).

SCALE OF FEMALE.—Length, 1 mm.; white, opaque. Exuviae pale yellowish.

FEMALE.—Usually one pair of *lobes* present (Plate 9, Fig. 2.), large, very prominent, crenate or serrate on the outer edges; number of crenations or teeth, five or six. Occasionally the second pair of lobes is represented by the merest rudiments of lobes. The *gland-spines* are arranged as follows, 1, 1, 1, 1, 1-2. They are quite long and slender. In addition to the ordinary *gland-spines* are other spines almost precisely like them in shape and appearance, but not supplied with the long tubular gland-ducts leading through them. These are prolongations of the prominences on which are located the marginal gland-orifices. See Plate 9, Fig. 4. The *dorsal gland-orifices* are numerous and conspicuous. First and second rows absent. Third row with 3—8 orifices in the anterior and 7—9 in the posterior group. Fourth row with 6—9 orifices in the anterior and 6—8 in the posterior group. In addition to these gland-orifices are numerous others which are much smaller and less conspicuous. These seem to have no very definite arrangement but are most numerous in the space between the lobes and the circumgenital gland-orifices. Median group of *circumgenital gland-orifices* numbering 9—14; anterior laterals, 22—26; posterior laterals, 16—18.

SCALE OF MALE.—Length about 1 mm. Rather irregular in form and feebly carinated.

MALE.—" Adult male bright reddish ; of normal form. Terminal joint of antenna shorter than ninth ; broad at base ; the narrowed apical portion conspicuously darker after staining ; a curved knobbed hair at apex. Foot with three digitules, one on claw and two on tarsus. Length including genital sheath, .75 mm." (Green).

REMARKS.

Found in Ceylon in the small pits at the base of the veins on the under surface of the leaves of *Elaeocarpus amoenus.* The number in a single pit varies from one to many. Where several are crowded into one pit they lose the elongated shape usual in this genus and become irregular in form.

HEMICHIONASPIS RHODODENDRI.

Chionaspis rhododendri Green, Coccidae of Ceylon, Part II., p. 119 (1899).

SCALE OF FEMALE.—Plate 3, Fig. 9. Length, 1.2—1.5 mm. More or less elongated, decidedly broadened posteriorly, sometimes being nearly as broad as long. Very thin and delicate in texture ; white or very pale yellow. Exuviae .5—.8 mm. long, pale brownish yellow or almost colorless.

FEMALE.—Elongated, segmentation moderately distinct. Median *lobes* (Plate 9, Fig. 7), large and conspicuous, only slightly colored ; the exposed edge of each lobe divided into about five obscure crenations. Second lobe very obscure or absent ; third lobe absent. *Gland-spines* short and almost conical in form. They are arranged as follows : 1, 1, 1, 1, 2-4. *Dorsal gland-orifices* few in number. Second row absent ; third and fourth rows represented only by their posterior groups each containing 1—3 orifices. Median group of *circumgenital gland-orifices* numbering 6—9 ; anterior laterals, 11—15 ; posterior laterals, 11—15.

SCALE OF MALE.—Plate 9, Fig. 9 A. Length, .8—1 mm. Plainly tri-carinate. Exuvia pale yellow or colorless.

Found in Ceylon on the under surface of the leaves of *Rhododen-
dron arboreum*. The insects are hidden beneath the densely felted
hairs of the under surface of the leaves and can be detected only by
the small yellow discolored spots on the upper surface. Mr. Green
states that a very large proportion are destroyed by parasites.

HEMICHIONASPIS DRACAENAE n. sp.

SCALE OF FEMALE.—Plate 2, Fig. 9. Length, 1.3—1.6 mm.
Pyriform, thin and delicate in texture ; white. Exuviae .6 mm. long,
brownish in color.

FEMALE.—Broad, nearly oval in outline, feebly segmented.
Median *lobes* (Plate 9, Fig. 1.) quite long and narrow, irregularly
crenate, usually slightly separated along their inner edges. Lobules
of the second pair small and inconspicuous. Third pair wanting.
The *gland-spines* are arranged as follows : 1, 1, 1, 1, 3. The *marginal
gland-orifices* are quite conspicuous, the first one being placed on a
broad prominence. The *dorsal gland-orifices* are very few in number
and can scarcely be reduced to a formula. Median group of *circumgenital gland-orifices*, 6—7 ; anterior laterals, 11—12 ; posterior laterals, 9—11.

SCALE OF MALE.—Plate 2, Fig. 9 A. Length, .8 mm. Delicate
in texture, feebly uni-carinate. Exuvia yellowish-brown, occupying
nearly one-half the length of the scale.

On *Dracaena cinnabari* from Socotia Island. Sent to the Department of Agriculture by Mr. W. S. MacDougall of Edinburgh, Scotland.

Explanation of Plate 1.

Fig. 1.   Female scale of *Hemichionaspis mussaendae*.

Fig. 1 A.   Male scale of the same species.

Fig. 2.   Female scale of *Hemichionaspis lata*, drawn from a cotype. *H. lata* is now considered a synonym of *H. aspidistrae*.

Fig. 3.   Female scale of *Hemichionaspis theae*.

Fig. 3 A.   Male scale of the same species.

Fig. 4.   Female scale of *Hemichionaspis aspidistrae*.

Fig. 4 A.   Male scale of the same species.

PLATE I.

1

1A

2

3A

3

4

4A

Explanation of Plate 2.

Fig. 1.   Female scale of *Chionaspis corni*.

Fig. 1 A.   Male scale of the same species.

Fig. 2.   Female scale of *Chionaspis longiloba*.

Fig. 2 A.   Male scale of the same species.

Fig. 3.   Female scale of *Chionaspis caryae*.

Fig. 3 A.   Male scale of the same species.

Fig. 4.   Female scale of *Chionaspis pinifoliae* (narrow form).

Fig. 4 A.   Male scale of the same species.

Fig. 4 B.   Female scale of *Chionaspis pinifoliae* (broad form).

Fig. 5.   Female scale of *Chionaspis wistariae*.

Fig. 5 A.   Male scale of the same species.

Fig. 6.   Female scale of *Chionaspis americana*.

Fig. 6 A.   Male scale of the same species.

Fig. 7.   Female scale of *Chionaspis furfura*.

Fig. 7 A.   Male scale of the same species.

Fig. 8.   Female scale of *Chionaspis salicis*.

Fig. 8 A.   Male scale of the same species.

Fig. 9.   Female scale of *Hemichionaspis dracaenae*.

Fig. 9 A.   Male scale of the same species.

PLATE II.

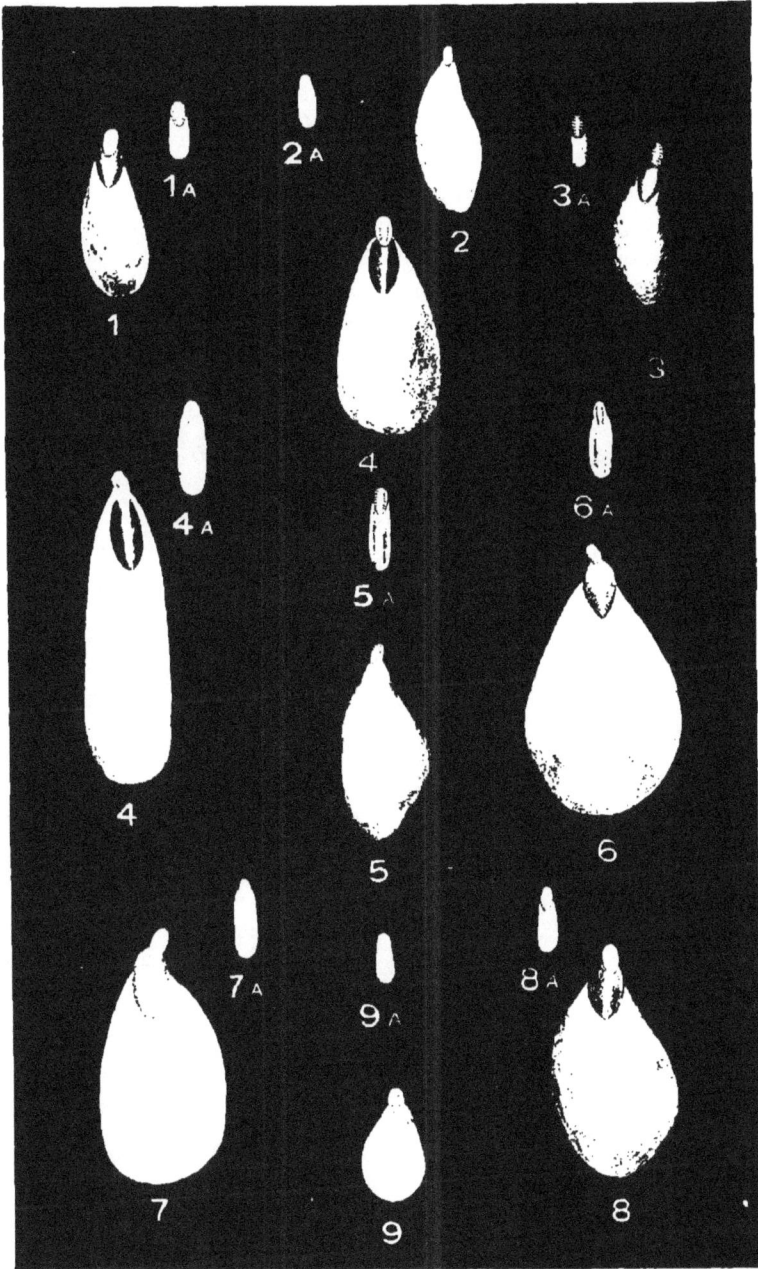

Explanation of Plate 3.

Fig. 1. Female scale of *Chionaspis salicis-nigrae.*

Fig. 1 A. Male scale of the same species.

Fig. 2. Female scale of *Chionaspis platani.*

Fig. 2 A. Male scale of the same species.

Fig. 3. Female scale of *Chionaspis lintneri.*

Fig. 3 A. Male scale of the same species.

Fig. 4. Female scale of *Hemichionaspis minor.*

Fig. 4 A. Male scale of the same species.

Fig. 5. Female scale of *Chionaspis herbae.*

Fig. 5 A. Male scale of the same species.

Fig. 6. Female scale of *Chionaspis dysoxyli.*

Fig. 6 A. Male scale of the same species.

Fig. 7. Female scale of *Chionaspis stanotophri.*

Fig. 7 A. Male scale of the same species.

Fig. 8. Female scale of *Chionaspis ortholobis.*

Fig. 8 A. Male scale of the same species.

Fig. 9. Female scale of *Hemichionaspis rhododendri.*

Fig. 9 A. Male scale of the same species.

PLATE III.

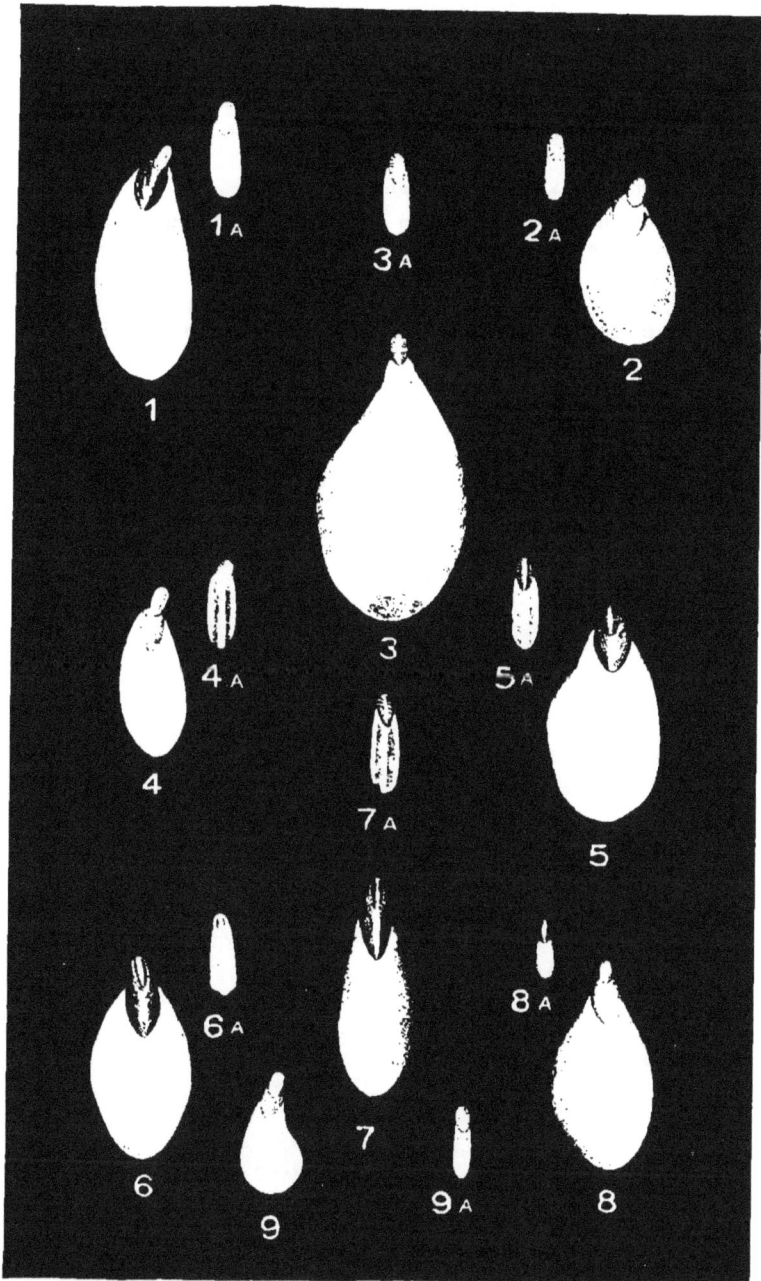

Explanation of Plate 4.

Fig. 1. Portion of the edge of the pygidium of *Fiorinia fioriniae* showing the median " notch " formed by the median lobes.

Fig. 2. Pygidium of *salicis*, the type of the genus Chionaspis.

Fig. 3. Portion of the edge of the pygidium of *Parlatoria* sp. The drawing is designed to show the type of " plates " found in the genus *Parlatoria*.

Fig. 4. Same from a species of *Aspidiotus*.

Fig. 5. Diagramatic representation of a pygidium, drawn to explain the form of description used in this paper. A, circumgenital gland-orifices. B, anterior groups of dorsal gland-orifices. C, posterior groups of dorsal gland-orifices. D, anus. E, marginal gland-orifices. F, spines of the dorsal surface. G, spines of the ventral surface. H, gland-spines. J, marginal gland-prominence. K, median lobes. L, second lobe. M, third lobe. N, genital orifice.

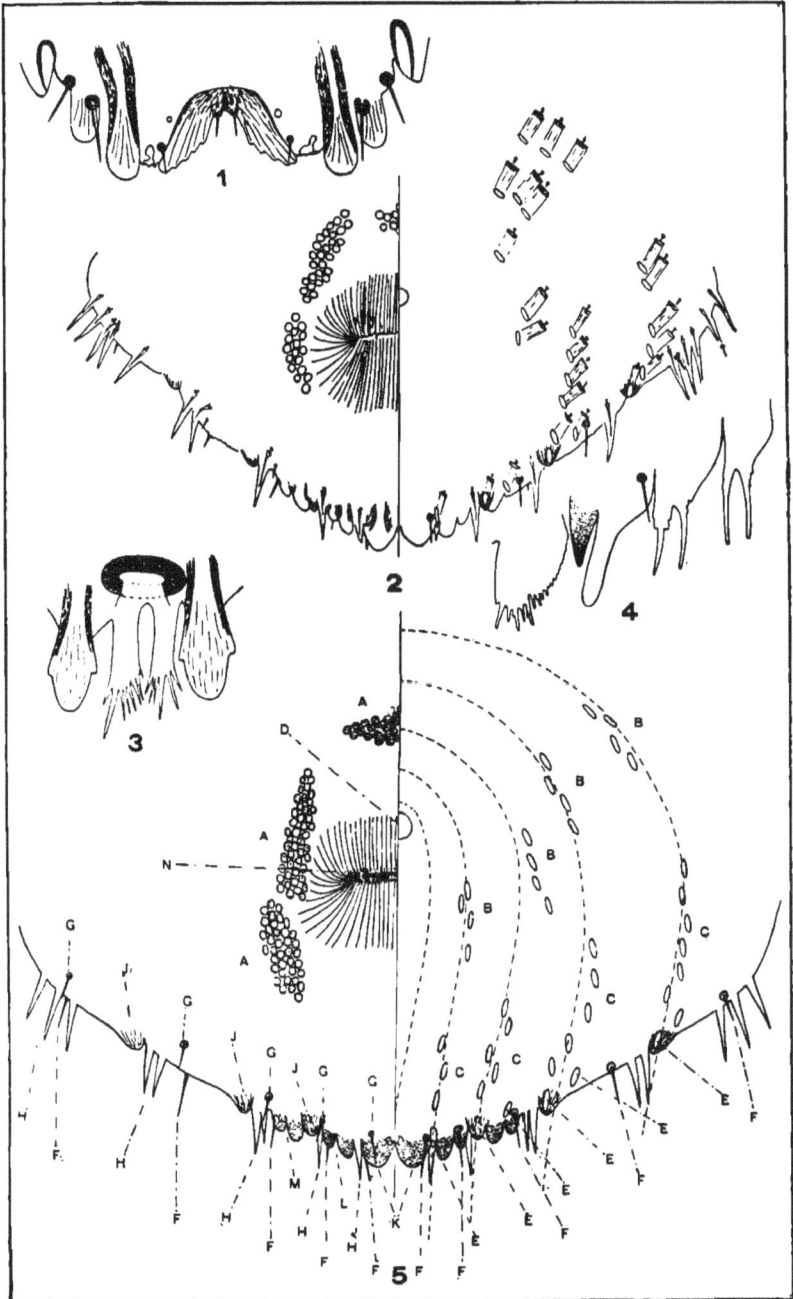

PLATE IV.

Explanation of Plate 5.

Fig. 1. Cross section of male scale of *Chionaspis salicis*.

Fig. 2. Leg of larva of *Chionaspis salicis*.

Fig. 3. Pygidium of *Chionaspis furfura*.

Fig. 4. Diagramatic representation of a female *Chionaspis* to show how the thirteen segments of the body may be accounted for.

Fig. 5. Larva of *Chionaspis americana* soon after it has come to rest : showing the way it begins the formation of the scale.

Fig. 6. Antenna of larva of *Chionaspis salicis*.

Fig. 7. Side view of female scale of *Chionaspis salicis*.

Fig. 8. Body of the female of *Chionaspis salicis*.

PLATE V.

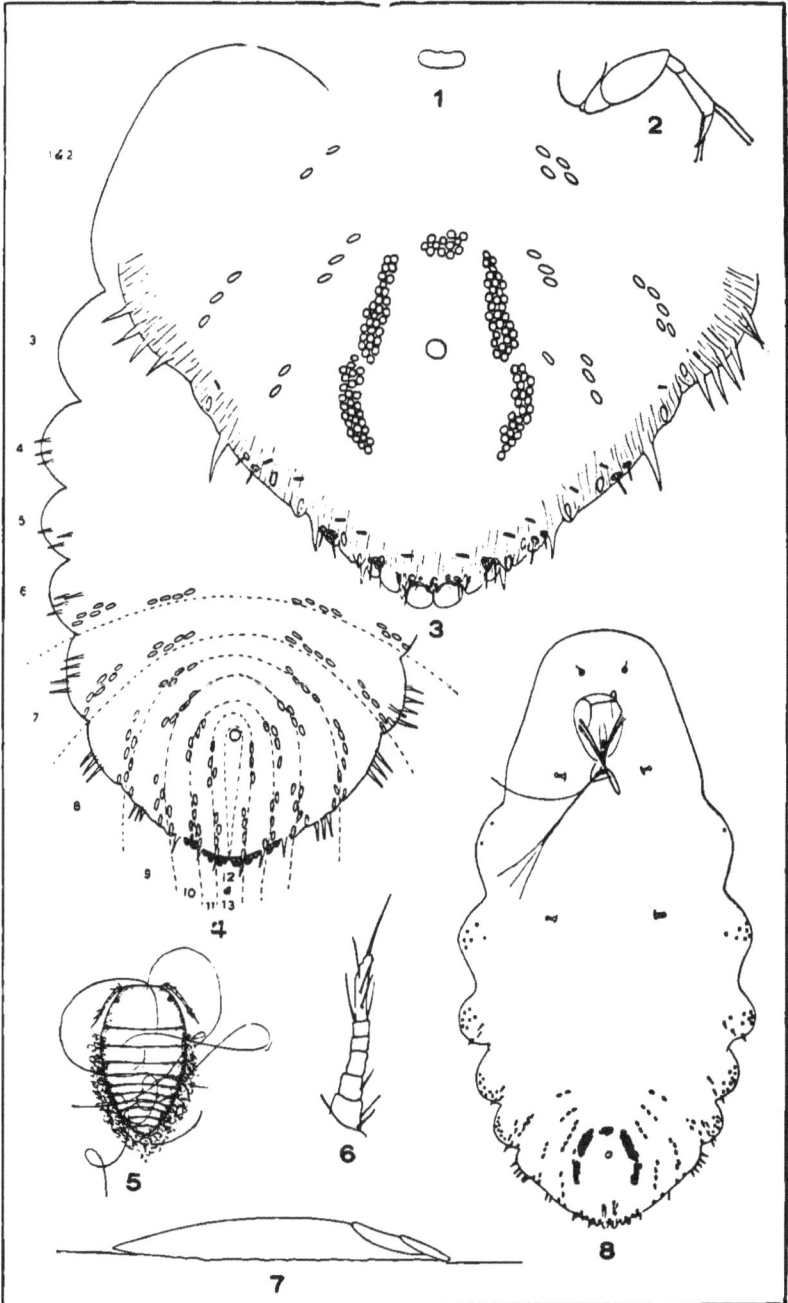

Explanation of Plate 6.

Fig. 1. Body of female of *Hemichionaspis aspidistrae*.

Fig. 2. Exuviae of *Hemichionaspis aspidistrae*.

Fig. 3. Same of *Hemichionaspis theae*.

Fig. 4. Edge of one of the abdominal segments of *Hemichionaspis theae*.

Fig. 5. A gland-spine from *Hemichionaspis aspidistrae*.

Fig. 6. Portion of body of *Hemichionaspis aspidistrae* showing the very prominent abdominal segments.

Fig. 7. Cross section of male scale of *Hemichionaspis aspidistrae*.

Fig. 8. Portion of body of *Hemichionaspis minor*.

Fig. 9. Pygidium of *Hemichionaspis aspidistrae*. The right side is a ventral and the left side a dorsal view.

Fig. 10. A gland-spine from *Hemichionaspis rhododendri*: the form which occurs on the abdominal segments.

PLATE VI.

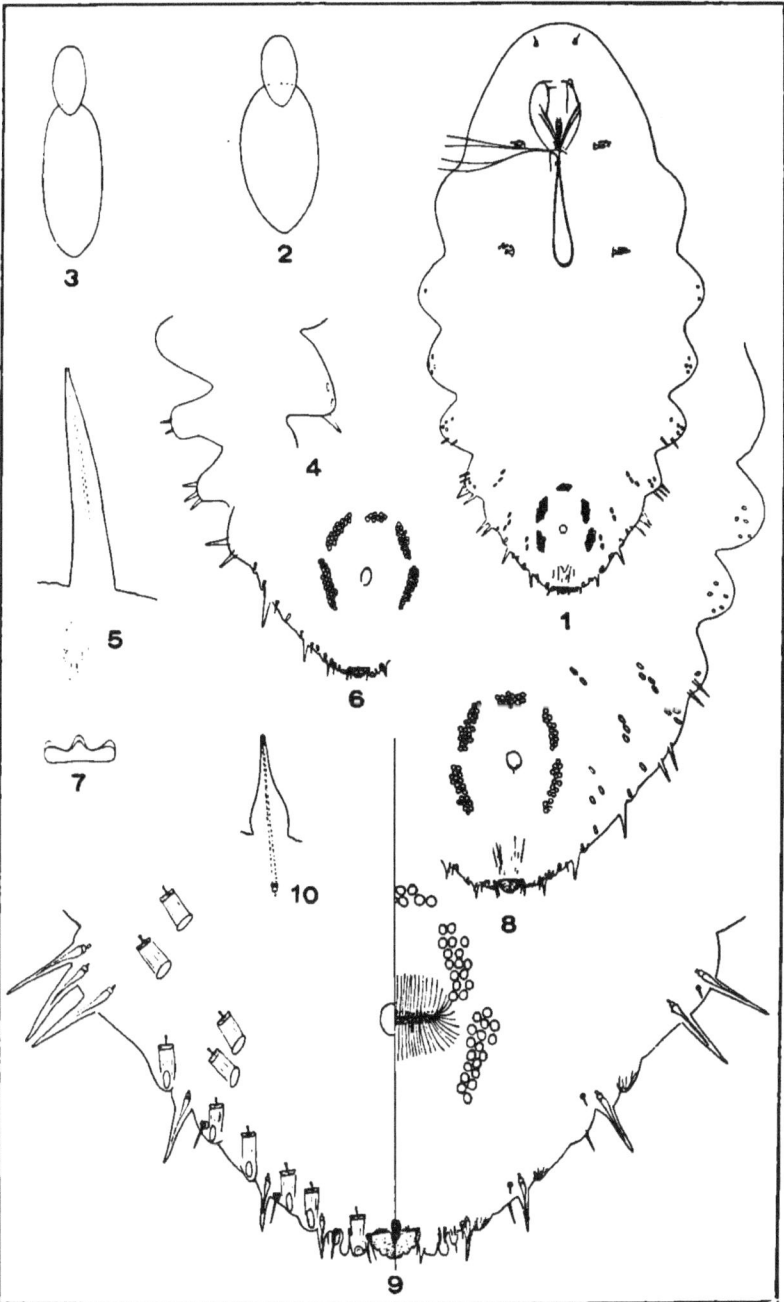

Explanation of Plate 7.

Portion from the edge of the pygidium of different species.

Fig. 1.   *Chionaspis salicis.*

Fig. 2.   *Chionaspis herbae.*

Fig. 3.   *Chionaspis salicis-nigrae.*

Fig. 4.   *Chionaspis pinifoliae heterophyllae.*

Fig. 5.   *Chionaspis platani.*

Fig. 6.   Second lobe of *Chionaspis platani* showing variation.

Fig. 7.   *Chionaspis wistariae.*

Fig. 8.   *Chionaspis pinifoliae.*

Fig. 9.   *Chionaspis lintneri.*

PLATE VII.

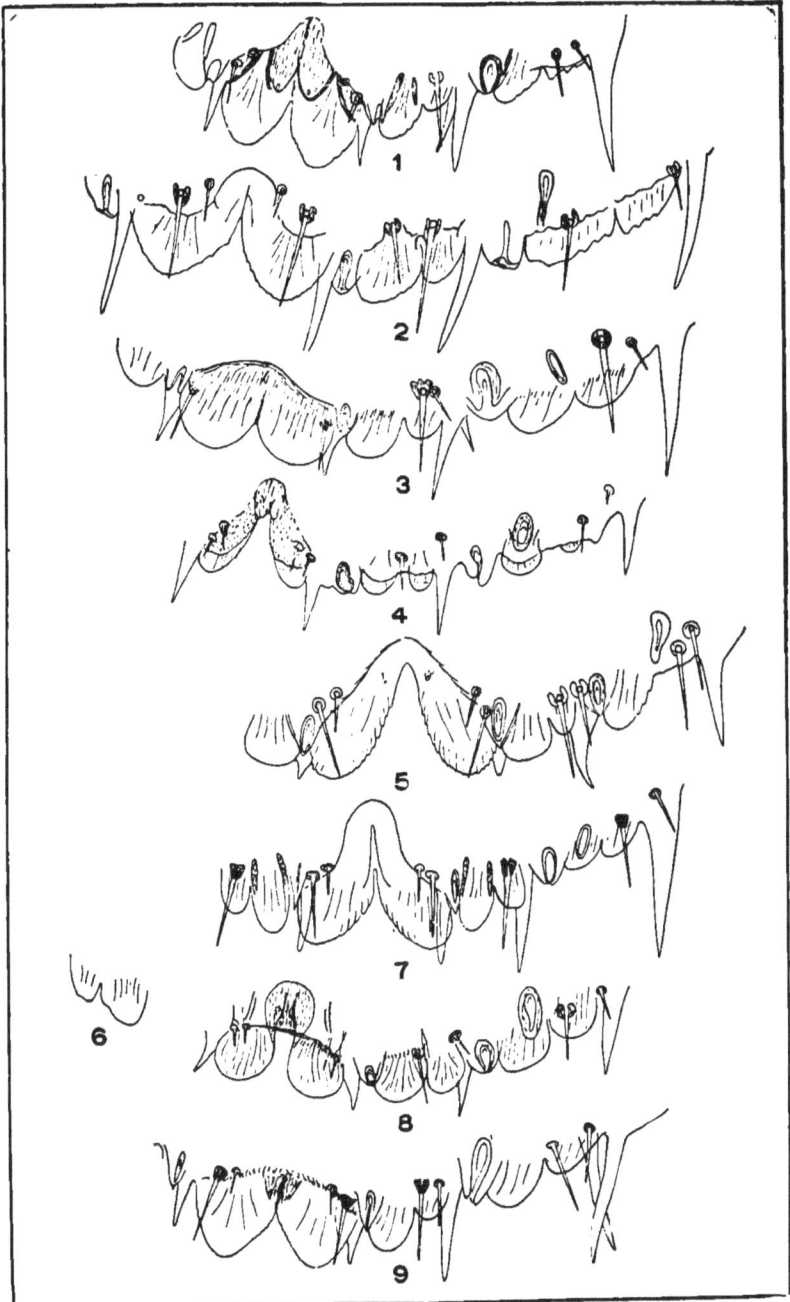

Explanation of Plate 8.

Portion of the edge of the pygidium of different species.

Fig. 1. *Chionaspis dysoxyli.*

Fig. 2. *Chionaspis ortholobis.*

Fig. 3. *Chionaspis americana.*

Fig. 4. Second lobe of *Chionaspis americana* showing variation.

Fig. 5. *Chionaspis caryae.*

Fig. 6. *Chionaspis furfura.*

Fig. 7. *Chionaspis longiloba.*

Fig. 8. *Chionaspis corni.*

Fig. 9. *Chionaspis stanotophri.*

PLATE VIII.

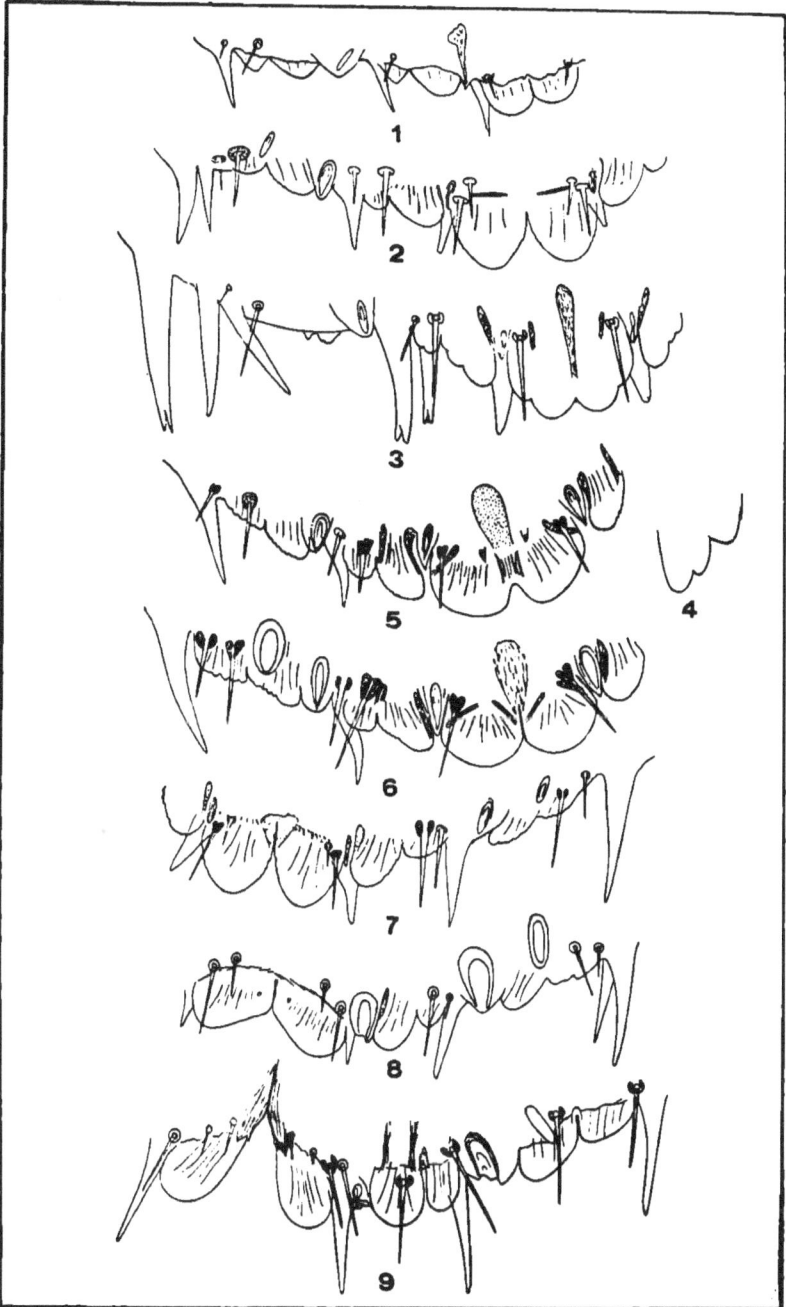

Explanation of Plate 9.

Fig. 1. Portion of edge of pygidium of *Hemichionaspis dracaenae*.

Fig. 2. Portion of edge of pygidium of *Hemichionaspis scrobicularum*.

Fig. 3. Portion of edge of pygidium of *Hemichionaspis theae*.

Fig. 4. Marginal gland prominence from *Hemichionaspis scrobicularum* showing how the edge is drawn out into a spine, resembling a gland-spine.

Fig. 5. Portion of edge of pygidium of *Hemichionaspis minor*.

Fig. 6. Median lobes of *Hemichionaspis minor strachani*.

Fig. 7. Portion of edge of pygidium of *Hemichionaspis rhododendri*.

Fig. 8. Median lobes of *Hemichionaspis aspidistrae* showing variation.

Fig. 9. Portion of edge of pygidium of *Hemichionaspis aspidistrae*.

Fig. 10. Portion of edge of pygidium of *Hemichionaspis mussaendae*.

Fig. 11. Portion of edge of pygidium of *Hemichionaspis minor* showing second lobe quite well developed.

Fig. 12. Dorsal gland-orifice of *Hemichionaspis scrobicularum*.

Fig. 13. Dorsal gland-orifice of the smaller variety from *Hemichionaspis scrobicularum*.

PLATE IX.

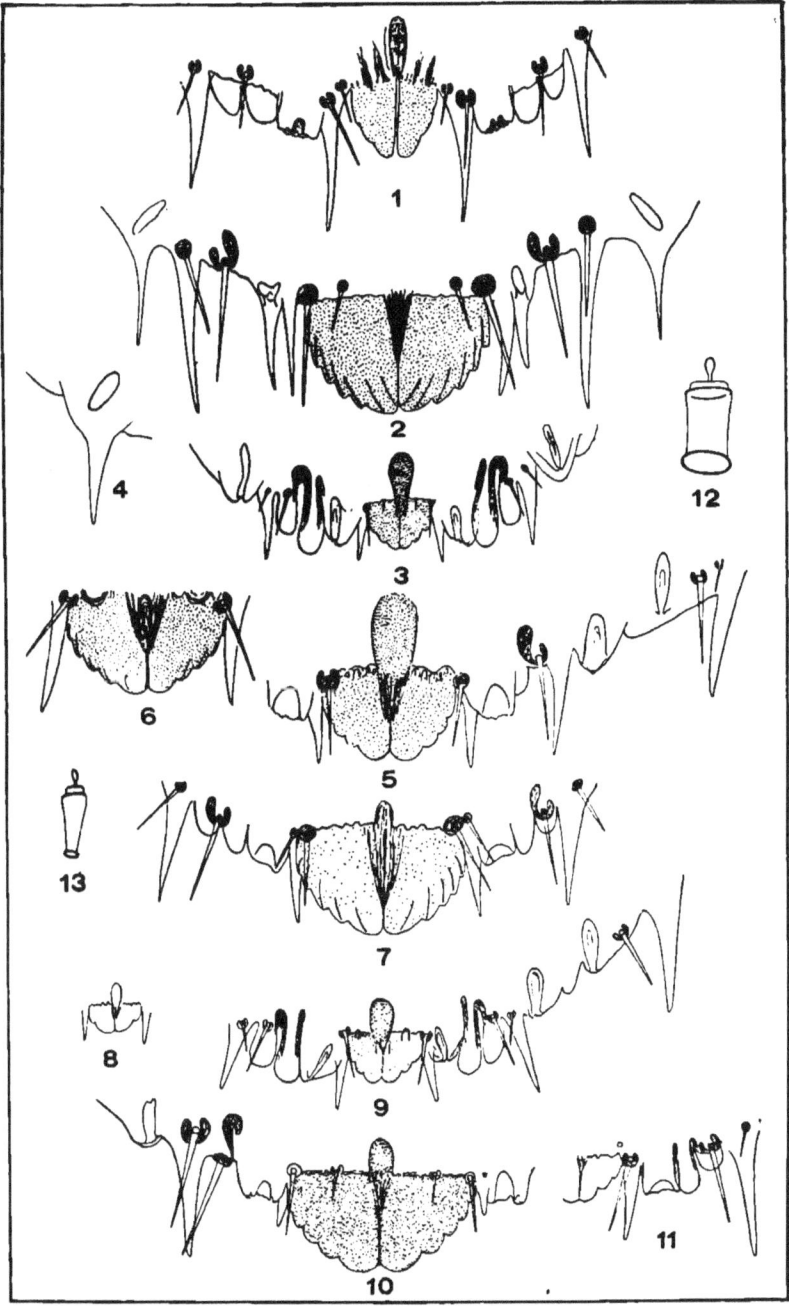

INDEX OF GENERA.

INDEX OF SPECIES AND VARIETIES.